TREE ᵀᴴᴱ LIFE
OF
ORACLE

TREE ^THE^ OF LIFE ORACLE

CHERRY GILCHRIST AND **GILA ZUR**

Card illustrations by Helen Jones

OH EDITIONS

*The Tree of Life Oracle in its present
form is dedicated to the Sentinels.*

This edition published by OH Editions
An imprint of the Welbeck Publishing Group
20 Mortimer Street London W1T 3JW

Text copyright © Cherry Gilchrist 2002
Card illustrations copyright © Helen Jones 2002
Design © Welbeck Non-Fiction Limited,
part of Welbeck Publishing Group Limited 2021

The right of Cherry Gilchrist and Gila Zur to be identified as the
authors of the work has been asserted by them in accordance with
the Copyright, Designs and Patents Act 1988.

All rights reserved. No part of this book may be reproduced, stored
in a retrieval system, or transmitted in any form or by any means
without the prior written permission of the publisher, nor be
otherwise circulated in any form of binding or cover other than
that in which it is published and without a similar condition being
imposed on the subsequent purchaser.

British Library Cataloguing-in-Publication data available on request.

ISBN 978 1 91431 726 2

10 9 8 7 6 5 4 3 2 1

Printed in China

CONTENTS

INTRODUCTION 6

The Kabbalah and the Tree of Life 8

The Origins of the Oracle 11

THE CARDS 14

The Wheels 15	5 The Dancer 58	10 Agitation 96
1 The Beloved 22	5 The Advisor 60	10 The Martyr 98
1 The Servant 24	6 Pandora's Box ... 62	10 The Presence 100
1 The Seed 26	6 Applause 64	11 The Return 102
1 The Head 28	6 The Edge 66	11 The Cauldron ... 104
2 The Sleeper 30	6 The Surgeon 68	11 Man of Blood ... 106
2 The Drunkard 32	7 The Heart 70	11 The Veil 108
2 Thirst 34	7 The Warrior 72	12 The Gambler ... 110
2 The Uprooted ... 36	7 The Victor 74	12 Concern 112
3 The Actor 38	7 The Treasury 76	12 Pride 114
3 The Coward 40	8 The Marker 78	12 The Society 116
3 The Observer 42	8 The Thaw 80	13 The Tempter 118
3 The Moment 44	8 The Test 82	13 The Sorrow 120
4 The Locksmith 46	8 The Sign 84	13 The Audience ... 122
4 The Eater 48	9 The Disciple 86	13 The Myth 124
4 The Witness 50	9 The Passover 88	14 The Covering ... 126
4 The Wanderer 52	9 The Flag 90	14 The Well 128
5 The Skeleton 54	9 The Court 92	14 The Point 130
5 The Sluggard 56	10 The Benefactor ... 94	14 Causality 132

READING THE CARDS 134

The Tree of Life and the Reading Sheet 136

How to Lay Out a Reading 138

Sample Reading 140

Acknowledgements 144

INTRODUCTION

An oracle provides a way to consult a source of wisdom and knowledge. It mediates for us between higher and lower worlds, and between our personal lives and a greater living presence in the universe. This particular oracle is designed not so much to give us all the answers, but to help us to ask the right questions, to glimpse possibilities and to understand how life may be unfolding.

The Oracle is based on the Kabbalah and its central symbol, the Tree of Life. The Kabbalistic Tree of Life is a stylized version of the Tree of Life symbol found in practically every culture, from motifs woven into oriental rugs to Native American totem poles and tales of Norse mythology. Just as the Oracle acts as a channel mediating between the worlds, so the Tree of Life is also a crystalline ladder which spans both the material and spiritual levels of existence. Seekers and sages through the centuries have devised such symbols to help us to understand the connection between the sacred and the everyday experience.

The Oracle arises out of the Tree, and uses its pathways, its spheres, or 'sefirot', and its philosophy. It is rooted in the twenty-two letters of the Hebrew alphabet, which are associated with the

Tree. It is true to the spirit of Kabbalistic teaching, but it has been newly developed and re-interpreted for the modern age.

Both the Oracle and the Tree are highly structured, because, as even the most inspired mystic knows, there is principle and harmony of order in this world of ours. This framework helps to orientate us, for although there is a place for intuition in divination, it is always best to have a language through which an oracle can speak.

Divination can give us a new outlook; it can bring comfort and insight, or even point disconcertingly to hidden truths. Sometimes it also sheds light on the future, but it is not used only for that purpose. An all-round, 360-degree perspective on the current situation may be more useful than a telescopic glimpse into the far distance.

Kabbalah is a living tradition and much of its wisdom is passed down orally or concealed in its symbols and teaching structures. The original 'creators' of this oracle claim only to have re-discovered it, and say that the knowledge it contains was waiting to be revealed in the placing of the Hebrew letters on the Tree of Life.

INTRODUCTION

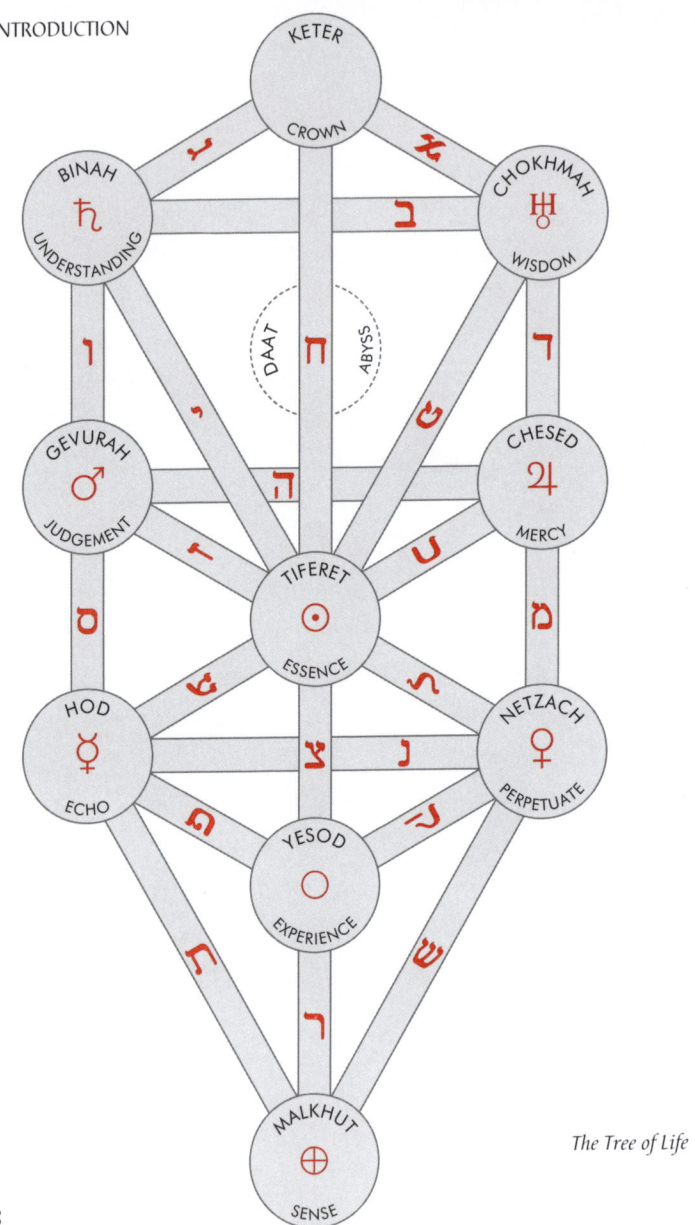

The Tree of Life

The Kabbalah and the Tree of Life

The Kabbalah is a mystical tradition that lies at the heart of Judaism. Its known origins go back to medieval times, when it emerged in Provence and Spain, but it is likely that its teachings extend further back by at least several centuries, and it perhaps evolved out of the wisdom schools of Assyria, Babylonia and Egypt. Stylized Tree of Life diagrams, very similar to that used here, can be found as stone carvings from these cultures, and other related traditions, such as astrology, have also passed along this route. Astrology and Kabbalah are close companions, and this oracle pack makes use of the planets, houses and zodiac signs of astrology, especially in the layout of the cards.

Kabbalah passed into European culture during the Renaissance, becoming one of the most important Western mystical philosophies from that time onwards. It also evolved further within Jewish teaching, and is increasingly practised as a way of understanding sacred cosmology.

Kabbalah maps out the pathways between man and God. The gulf between us is not a hopeless, uncharted wilderness, in fact, creation is a process of step-by-step revelation, aided by Kabbalah's greatest symbol, the Tree of Life, which shows us how the cosmic principles operate, and how they can be found at work within everything, including the individual person.

The Tree of Life begins with Keter, the Crown of Creation, the highest source of divine energy that we can know. The path of creation follows a course known as the Lightning Flash, zigzagging from right to left (*see page 12*), and as it does so, it sets up three pillars, the three vertical supports of the Tree of Life. Each pillar has its own meaning: the right-hand one is masculine, creative and expansive; the left-hand, feminine side, forms and shapes. The central pillar balances the other two, and is known as the Pillar of Consciousness. As creation unfolds, ten sefirot, or emanations of divine energy, appear. From Keter the path leads to

Chokhmah, sphere of Wisdom, also known as the Father, and then to Binah, the great Mother and source of Understanding. These three are known as the supernal triad; we can access their powers, but not master or own them. Creation then passes across Daat, the sefira that 'is and is not', often known as the Abyss or the Gate. This marks the entry point to the human world, at the exalted level of Chesed (Loving-Kindness or Mercy) and Gevurah (Judgement). Tiferet, called variously Essence, Adornment and Knowledge, is at the heart of the human world, the place where we know our own identity and value. Netzach (Perpetuate) is the realm of everyday feelings and desires, which constantly renew themselves, and Hod (Echo) is our apparatus for communication. Yesod is called Experience or the Foundation. Here, the personality is established so that we can function and interact properly. Finally, we reach Malkhut, called Sense, otherwise known as the Kingdom. This is the level of physical matter, known more poetically as the garden where the Holy Feminine Spirit resides.

Now the Tree is complete: ten sefirot have manifested themselves, connected by twenty-two paths. The Hebrew alphabet, which has twenty-two letters, is usually assigned to these paths. There are other attributions too, and because the Tree has been used by different cultures and for different purposes, it has gathered a wealth of correspondences, including colours, symbols, planets, virtues and vices, and governing angels. The Tree of Life also contains four worlds which signify four different levels of experience: briefly, these are the world of matter, centred on Malkhut; the world of image and flow, centred on Yesod; the world of angels and creation, centred on Tiferet; and the world of emanation and archetype which exists at the topmost triad on the Tree.

This is a condensed introduction to the Tree of Life. There are many ways of working with this symbol, including study groups, meditation, magical and ritual practice, and practical application in everyday life. It is one of the most remarkable and adaptable symbols ever created.

The Origins of the Oracle

In London, in the early 1970s, two Kabbalists were working on a problem that had intrigued Kabbalists for centuries: How should they place the twenty-two Hebrew letters on the twenty-two paths of the Tree of Life? There were various existing ways of numbering the paths, but none of these satisfied the researchers. It has always been taught that the Hebrew alphabet is sacred and that divine secrets are contained within its letters. The letters can be meditated upon and when they are arranged into words in a meaningful way, inner and more profound meanings can be found by combining those letters in different orders, which in turn gives different words. Number and letter are also aligned in Hebrew. This technique, often known as 'permutation', or Gematria, is a key practice in Kabbalah, and has often been used to study the Old Testament. It was especially well-known under the great thirteenth-century Kabbalist Abraham Abulafia, who taught his students to meditate upon the letters.

Following this principle, the researchers tried a new scheme by placing the letters on the Tree of Life in the order of the descent of the Lightning Flash, and the new paths that are created between the sefirot in its wake (shown in the diagram overleaf).

Then they began experimenting to see how these letters would combine on local, self-contained sections of the Tree – the 'wheels' that appear on the cards of the Oracle. To their surprise, these clusters of Hebrew letters formed numerous significant words, whereas other accepted arrangements of the letters on the Tree were almost completely unfruitful.

Thus a complete divination system began to reveal itself. Fourteen wheels in all were taken from the Tree, each with a sefira from the central Pillar of Consciousness at its heart. Four different words were selected for each wheel, and each was assigned to one of the four

INTRODUCTION

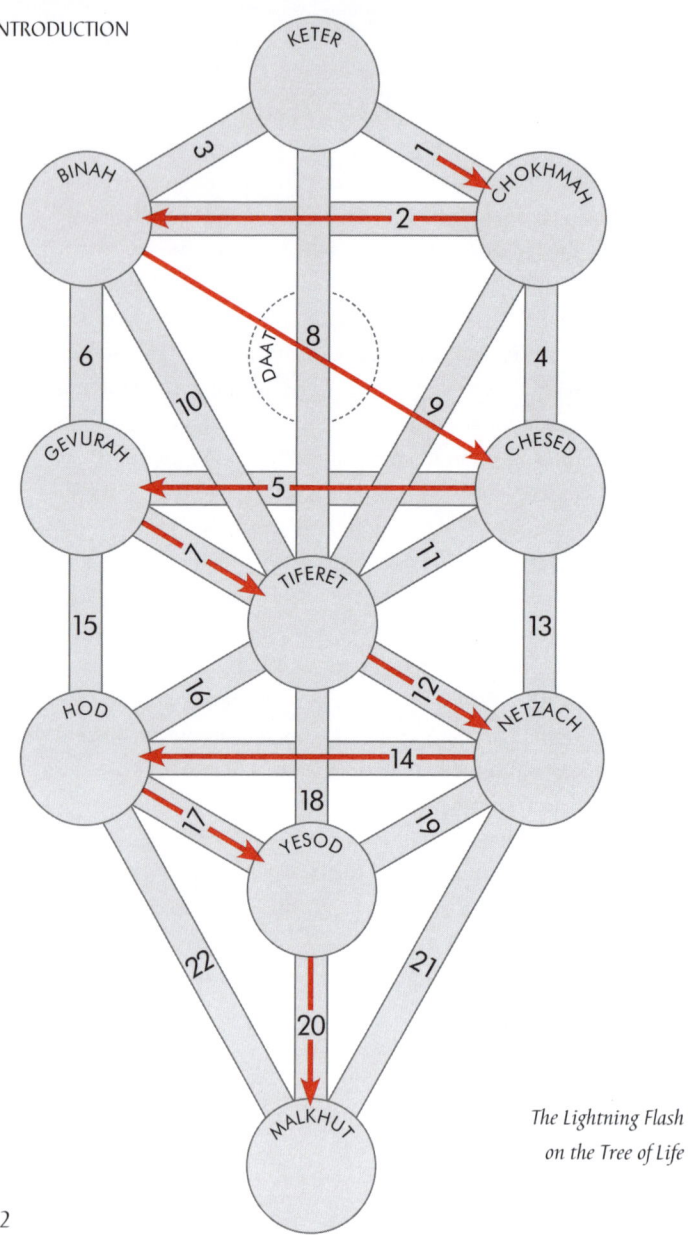

The Lightning Flash on the Tree of Life

THE ORIGINS OF THE ORACLE

elements, similar to the four suits of other card decks. This created fifty-six named emblems, the cards of the Oracle. A layout for reading the cards was devised, based on the Tree of Life and its astrological correspondences. It appears on the reading sheet in this pack, along with the connections with the Tree of Life diagram, and the meanings and time frame of each astrological house card position. A fifty-seventh blank card was added, to ensure readings were valid. The divination system was now essentially complete.

It was known as Galgal, which means 'wheels', and was used in private Kabbalistic circles for many years. It is now receiving a new life in this current, expanded oracle pack. I was one of the original authors who wrote the instructions for the first oracle, though not one of its creators. Gila Zur was a creator, and a fourth writer, Eddie Prevost, joined the team of the time to muse upon the emblems and to write meditations upon the cards. In this current version, I have adapted these to become the 'Oracle' section of each card and have added the 'Commentary' and 'Interpretations' to give a full and practical key to the cards.

Kabbalah means 'to receive'. The creators of this oracle received a new and illuminating teaching from their work with the Kabbalah. They held the door open for wisdom to enter. I have tried to do the same in my approach to the oracle. Kabbalah reveals its inner light, but it does so only when we question, explore, and investigate in the spirit of truth.

CHERRY GILCHRIST

THE CARDS

There are four suits of fourteen cards in the pack. Each card is a 'wheel' based on a segment of the Tree of Life. These wheels can easily be related to the Tree, although their shape has been adapted. Every wheel comes in four different aspects, each with a different name gleaned from the Hebrew letter combinations on their relevant paths, and so each card aspect is assigned to one of the four elements: earth, water, fire and air. These elements are similar to those in astrology, where earth signifies the practical, material level; water is emotional and changeable; fire is creative and energizing; and air is intellectual and abstract. They can also be looked at in connection with the four worlds on the Tree of Life, described briefly on page 10.

There is also a blank card, whose task it is to stop the reading if it is inappropriate to continue. You can find out more about this on page 139. In the final section of the book, you will also find complete instructions for laying out and reading the cards, with the help of the reading sheet included in the pack. You may wish to keep a record of your readings, so that you can refer back to them at a later date, or to see how the depth of insight can increase as you become more familiar with using the Oracle.

This section takes you through the cards one by one (pages 22–133), and can be used for reference during a reading. It begins with an introduction to the fourteen wheels.

Wheel 1

This is the only wheel which has Sense (Malkhut) at its centre. The physical world is at first sight the most obvious, but it is really the most mysterious and difficult to understand. What is matter? Bodies that are apparently solid reveal hidden universes – atoms, genes, molecules, sub-atomic particles. The further we go, the more our normal notions of time, space and matter disappear; the unknown awaits us when we pass through the gates of matter. Is our material world the same as it is for a bee, a bird or a worm? In Kabbalah, the lowest sefira of Malkhut is known as the sacred garden. It is the feminine spirit, and the manifestation of the divine to our senses. These cards refer to sensory input and how we process it, and also to the image of the garden with its fertile soil for new growth.

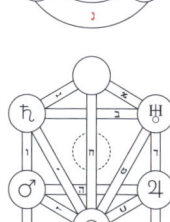

Wheel 2

Here we have the first of three sets of cards which are centred on Experience. This corresponds to the sefira of Yesod on the central pillar of the Tree of Life. Each wheel is governed by a sefira taken from the central pillar on the Tree of Life. This is the Pillar of Consciousness, and no living, changing situation can exist in human life without the presence of at least one of the sefirot from that pillar. Experience, or Yesod, governs much of our waking and sleeping lives; it is the realm of the personality, and the changing patterns of interaction. It is the place where we shape and process the impressions that we receive. This particular wheel formation takes us into an imaginative, responsive, but unstable level of experience, governed by flows of desire and reaction. That is why many of the cards of wheel 2 suggest a world of dreams and illusions.

THE CARDS

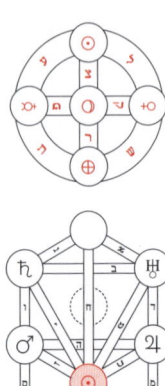

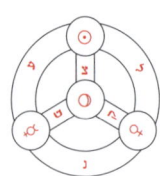

Wheel 3

The next set of four cards is also based on the realm of Experience, but here we have a quartet of outlying sefirot, instead of a volatile threefold wheel. This set is more stable because Tiferet, referred to as Essence, takes its place on the top rim of the wheel. Essence stands at the gateway between the personal world and the higher world, where the essence and principles of things can be perceived. The flow of Experience, symbolized by the waxing and waning moon, is grounded in Sense and illuminated by the calm solar radiance of Tiferet. As you can see from the oracles for these cards, this brings a certain glamour, but there is still a fine balance between alertness and illusion, between the manifestation of something and its loss or disappearance. The cards span a very human world, with its flashes of higher consciousness, its love of sensuality, and a certain degree of self-importance.

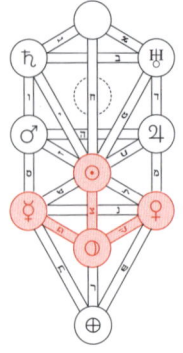

Wheel 4

Now the sefira of Sense, the external world, has been left behind, throwing the seeker back on their inner resources. These are still based on personal experience, but include resources that constellate around the central truth of one's being. The sefira of Tiferet represents the essential self. It has its individual perfection, but this may not mean perfection by human standards; each person's essence has its traits of character, such as avarice, impulsiveness or reticence. This is similar to the essential nature of an animal which may be predatory, slothful or excitable. We can rejoice in its nature because it is free from artifice. Discovering the inner light of Tiferet does not turn people into saints, which is just as well, since rumour has it that saints are hard to live with. Four very different types of people are described here, according to the four elements which rule each wheel.

Wheel 5

We have reached the level where Essence, or Tiferet, forms the centre of the wheel. This is the highest sefira that human life can be based in; above is Daat, the Abyss, which is a gateway to the supernal world and not strictly speaking a sefira at all, while the topmost sefira is Keter, the Crown of Creation. While we may have intimations of that Crown, we can never identify with it. To centre on Tiferet marks the entry into a level of self-awareness. Two opposing approaches arise at this stage, but they are in fact two sides of a golden coin. The first is stasis, revealed in two of the cards, because there is the temptation to bask in the light of one's essence and do nothing. The second is evolution, an impulse to movement that celebrates and transforms the energy at the heart of life.

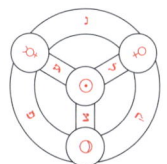

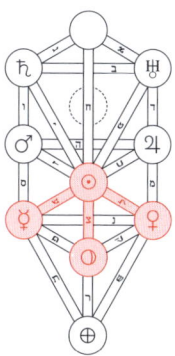

Wheel 6

The wheel now includes Judgement and Mercy, along with the sefirot of Gevurah and Chesed. On the Tree of Life, Chesed is created first. 'The world is tempered by Chesed, "Mercy", and is filled therewith.' The balance between judgement and mercy occupies a key place in human history. Poets, philosophers and playwrights have all struggled with the issue. Kabbalah tells us that both are necessary, but that the universe could not stay in existence without the presence of Loving-Kindness, another name for Chesed. When judgement has been exercised, what remains is love. This wheel brings this into a personal context, by including Experience.

These four cards contain ambiguity, the sense of standing on the edge between good and bad, health and disease, approval and condemnation. Duality can never entirely be denied, and we must recognize both the good that lies at the heart of tragedy and the dangers inherent in blessings.

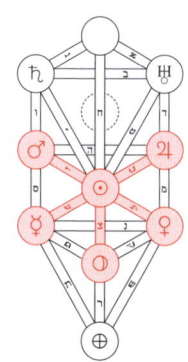

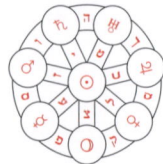

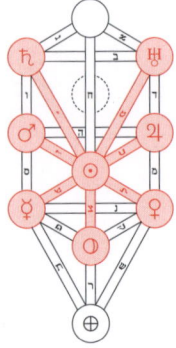

Wheel 7

Now we move to a set of cards with seven sefirot at the rim. Understanding (Binah) and Wisdom (Chokhmah) are the two highest spheres on the left- and right-hand pillars on the Tree of Life. They are beyond visible manifestation in everyday terms, though an individual may glimpse something of their profundity and power. Binah encompasses ultimate form, which equates with perfect understanding; Chokmah opens the way to wisdom, to a galaxy of possibilities in the fertile energy of the universe. They are Mother and Father, the Dark and the Light, the Form and the Force. The cards have an abundance which comes from having the courage to include these powers. They grant you the right to win life, to use its bounty and to triumph over difficulties, as long as you pay what is owed and acknowledge truth. From this point on, purity of purpose is needed.

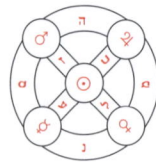

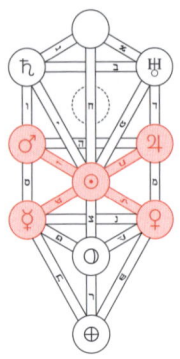

Wheel 8

From the sumptuous, sevenfold wheel of the last set, we come to a more honed and sparse wheel, containing only one sefira from the central pillar – the Pillar of Consciousness – which contains four sefirot: Malkhut (Sense), Yesod (Experience), Tiferet (Essence) and Keter (the Crown of Creation). Keter does not appear at the centre of a wheel, because it is a centre of divine, not human, consciousness. Malkhut as Sense only appears once at the centre, which means that the remaining interplay is very much between Tiferet, the essence of being, and Yesod, the personality. Where both appear, one at the centre and one on the rim, there is a certain amount of ambiguity and challenge, while any wheel, such as this, which contains only one of these sefirot, will be more clear-cut. Here the centre is Essence, and each card speaks of how we distinguish identity.

THE WHEELS

Wheel 9

Again Essence stands at the centre, surrounded by its loyal supporters, the six sefirot composing the outer rim of the wheel. And the meanings of the cards that carry this emblem relate to authority and allegiance. This wheel relates to confidence, the full blossoming of power that lies within human attainment, but it does not yet recognize the very highest source of power, Keter, the Crown, and it also stands aloof from the day-to-day concerns which are embodied in Experience and Sense. So the notion of being special and above reproach can also take hold. This set of cards does however carry the knowledge of that which joins a line together, a lineage of teaching, of authority, of identity stretching far back into history. Each of the elements bears witness to the contact between higher and lower, past and present.

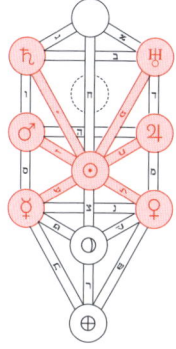

Wheel 10

A wind stirs the top of the tree; the whole tree shakes and trembles. Keter, the Crown, makes its appearance. Beyond the Crown, nothing is known. This is the highest presence we can ever experience. Those who thought they were in authority before the Crown appeared, now retreat to their proper places in the order of things below. Essence (Tiferet) supports its new lord with a stout heart, and Experience (Yesod) quivers with anticipation. This eightfold wheel is the fullest in the pack. It contains every sefira except for Sense (Malkhut). As a Significator in a reading, one of these cards suggests someone in full possession of their mental powers, with an understanding of the deeper levels of reality. However, every card must be read in its context, and in an everyday situation we may need to find a more mundane meaning for an individual card.

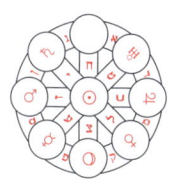

THE CARDS

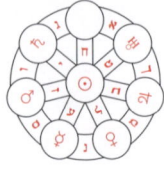

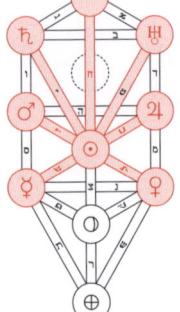

Wheel 11

From the maximum of eight sefirot at the rim of the wheel, we now return to seven, and from this point on through the remaining wheels of the pack, the number will diminish. Seven is still a high number, though, and these cards reflect the richness of that. They carry a quality of ripeness and maturity. They contain the distillation of experience, whether it is in the sacred relics of a temple or through the proud lineage of family life. Again, they take us beyond the span of an individual life to an essence of meaning created by generations, and by the patient workings of Nature and time. Tiferet, as Essence, is like the beauty of a song which has been sung by many voices through the generations, and which will be sung again and again, subtly changed by each voice, but never losing its essential message.

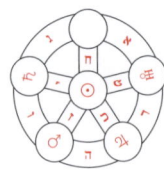

Wheel 12

This is a dynamic, fivefold wheel, where Tiferet sits in the centre of the five highest sefirot on the Tree of Life. It has access to the highest authority, to the triad of Crown, Wisdom and Understanding. The lower world of everyday interaction has been left behind. The wheel contains the whole kingdom of the upper world, including the path between Judgement and Mercy where, it is said, the armies of the Lord march to and fro. The person who knows this level of being is a commander, but must always remember whom he or she serves under. There are pitfalls in high places, especially when we overestimate our personal powers and do not attribute them to a source beyond ourselves. In the end, individual bids for supreme domination always fail. There is no place for sleepy negligence here either; this wheel demands wakeful attention at all times.

Wheel 13

This wheel focuses upon the four-square constellation of the sefirot Judgement, Mercy, Understanding and Wisdom, with Essence at their heart. This is an uncompromising set, with no recourse either to the highest of all for release or to the distractions of the imagination and senses. It is like a court, a place of higher judgement. As the oracles suggest, it is also a place of power but one where normal personal concerns are stripped away. There are dangers in this power, because here they don't have reference to the supreme authority, Keter, the Crown. Nor is the power tempered by the rebuffs and trivia of everyday life.

No one could live permanently within the arena created by these four sefirot. Even lingering here too long may give delusions of grandeur, and dislocate one from the proper concerns of daily life. It is the place of myth, ritual, meditation and intensive study.

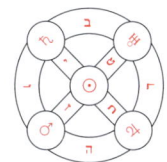

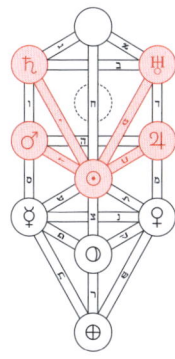

Wheel 14

This is the last set of wheels. We have moved steadily up the Tree of Life, taking in different groupings of the sefirot, linked together by the paths which act as conduits for the energy that the sefirot generate. Now we arrive at the highest point, where the Crown, Understanding and Wisdom, the topmost triad on the Tree, are placed on the wheel around Essence. This is the pinnacle of the creation as we know it, the highest world which governs the blueprints of creation and from which arise the deepest, unworded thoughts of the mind. But, of course, we have to use words and images to describe those thoughts. Even though these can only be symbols and tokens of a more potent reality. The Oracle is applied Kabbalah: these images help to guide us and to seek answers to both spiritual and more mundane questions.

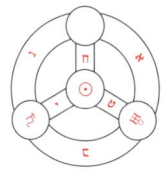

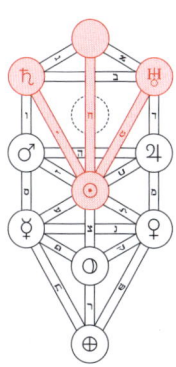

THE CARDS

The Beloved

פנק תשר

Wheel 1
Suit: EARTH
COMPANION CARDS:
*The Servant,
The Seed, The Head*

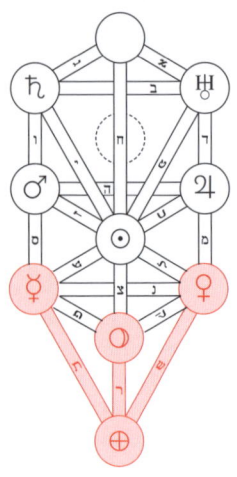

ORACLE

To make a gift of your life is the noblest of actions. But to truly give requires more than nobility. If you set aside will and responsibility, and offer yourself unconditionally, you are indulging yourself on a whim. Life itself demands discrimination – does not the body reject invasion, repelling all other bodies foreign to it? Therefore every act of giving must be in accordance with the nature of life. A sacrifice will only be of benefit if both the motives and the possible consequences are understood. Making the ultimate sacrifice, giving yourself to that which is truly beloved, must be done without self-indulgence. Giving without proper thought is the action of a spoilt child.

COMMENTARY

It is said that all creation is held in place by love, and if that love were withdrawn everything would disappear. Your body represents your connection with life; you inhabit it, you can choose whether to look after it or damage it, but you cannot create it. So your first commitment is to remember that the body is an expression of the fundamental creative impulse, a crystallized material form which gives us identity. Respect for this will go a long way towards relieving anxiety about our appearance and physique, and may also help us come to terms with illness.

If the body is formed from love we have a responsibility to use it in service to love and life. There are many ways in which this is done: in conceiving and bearing a child, in physical work, and in literally 'lending a hand' to others in need. We also give the body in physical love, not only sexually, but through the art of touch, massage and healing.

But this love is not sentimental. As the oracle says, it does not mean thoughtless self-sacrifice. This would be a waste, leading to needless destruction and perhaps creating a burden for others. We need to look after our bodies too, because neglecting them is also a kind of indulgent self-sacrifice. But nor does it mean an excess of self-love: constant preening and mirror-gazing blocks the flow of energy. Physical life is for sharing, but for sharing with discrimination. As the oracle says, the body needs to maintain its boundaries and its defence systems in order to stay healthy.

INTERPRETATIONS

Life tasks: *Do you pay enough attention to the physical world? Perhaps you need to strike up a dialogue with your body and your senses – listen to what they are telling you. But choose your course of action wisely, with love.*

Possible meanings: *Pregnancy. A renewal of physical energy. Cultivation of beauty. Treatment for ailments. Gardening, tending the environment. A lucky win or bonus. A loved one. A meeting after long absence.*

The Servant

נפק שרת

Wheel 1
Suit: WATER
COMPANION CARDS:
*The Beloved, The Seed,
The Head*

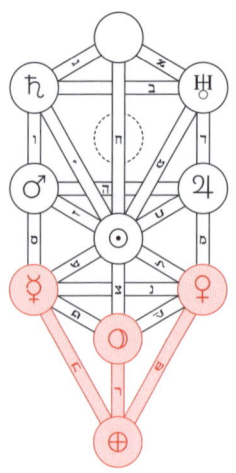

ORACLE
It is the servant's duty to carry out the requests of his or her master or mistress. He must be at one with his master, and act justly on his behalf, even when he is absent. The true servant does not need instructions, for he is capable of acting exactly as the master would wish, taking initiatives that his master would approve of. Yet at all times, the servant must maintain the relative positions of master and servant, for a servant who believes himself to have stepped into his master's shoes is a monster, and often a cruel one at that. So it is with our sense faculties; they are there to do all that is commanded and expected of them, without desiring to take control themselves.

COMMENTARY
Nowadays, it may be harder for us to contemplate a master-servant relationship, because we are used to a more egalitarian society. However, the relationship between employer and employee is similar. The employer needs to be confident, but not overbearing, and the employee mindful of the greater interests of the business. There is an appropriate structure of service and command, and this can mean that the employer will go

without in order to pay the employee's wages when times are bad. The employee works within the limited scope of his or her responsibility. But, as the oracle suggests, there is a real meaning of service here too, which goes beyond simply giving a fair return for the money.

The outward role of master or mistress, and servant, comprises the external meaning of this card. But the oracle leads us into the realm of the psyche, where the senses act as messengers and servants for the mind. The right relationship here is for the mind to receive and process the information provided by the senses, but not to be overwhelmed by it. A driver has to control his horses, and not let them run away with him. They respond to all sorts of stimuli, and if he is not careful, they can go off course with disastrous results. He has to be sensitive to how they are reacting, but be ready to reassure them and steer them firmly. It can seem exciting to let yourself go on a rush of sensation, but beware of where it may land you.

INTERPRETATIONS

Life tasks: *You can never work in isolation. There is always a source for your directives, and a recipient for their output. Where do you stand in the chain of command? Are you giving fair service, and are you handling your domain responsibly?*

Possible meanings: *A change of employment or a new project. An employment issue, in which you need to go beyond regulations and consider what is really just. An opportunity to give service. A flood of new impressions to be processed.*

THE CARDS

The Seed

נקף שתר

Wheel 1
Suit: FIRE
COMPANION CARDS:
*The Beloved,
The Servant, The Head*

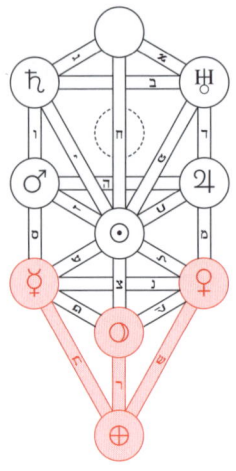

ORACLE

The seed contains all its history and all its future possibilities. But whereas the seed cannot be changed, the soil which receives it may be well-tilled or it may be neglected. In this soil, the seed will germinate, then grow to maturity, and generate seed in its own likeness. Then it will decay, leaving only the memory of its life within the new seed and the generations of seeds that come after.

What is your seed? Will you prepare the ground well for it? Store your memories, codify them, recognize them, so that they will enrich the soil. You can reproduce those memory sensations almost at will, to keep your earth turned and enlivened, a source of rich fertility for other seeds that may fall there.

COMMENTARY

A seed seems such a simple thing. But it contains a huge amount of programmed information. It also has a kind of volition, in that it has the will to germinate, sprout and grow, and thus to move forward in time. A seed is connected to all the plants that have preceded it, and to the future plants that will grow from it. This is why it is linked with fire in this set, because it is a kind of energy form.

If you think about your own position now, you can also extend this forwards and backwards in time. This means not only the physical, family line of your parents and your descendents, but also the lineage of your work or your spiritual path. You are shaped and inspired by the input of those who came before you, and you too will renew and recreate that impulse and pass it on to others.

As the oracle suggests, nothing is guaranteed. A seed can fall on barren land; this is also a part of nature, and sometimes we have to accept that we cannot go any further, whether it is physical infertility or a line of work or enquiry that has run its course. You can also teach another person, and see no apparent result. But it is always important to cultivate the garden. Whatever talents you have, you need to give them good soil to flourish in.

INTERPRETATIONS

Life tasks: *It helps to keep past and future in mind, but you can also consider every moment as a new beginning. There is always a seed waiting to be planted. Be ready to acknowledge what has gone into creating that seed, even though it is self-contained. You are the gardener too: look after the earth, and the first fragile growth there.*

Possible meanings: *An opportunity which needs cultivation. Your talents will be called upon. An issue about viability – whether something has got potential or is 'infertile'. Check your resources; know what you have at your disposal.*

The Head

רשת פקנ

Wheel 1
Suit: AIR

COMPANION CARDS:
The Beloved,
The Servant, The Seed

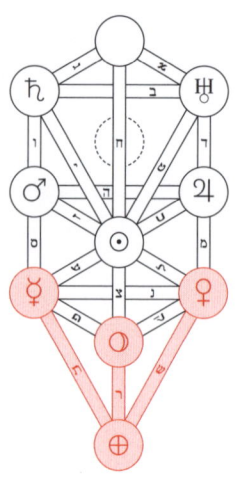

ORACLE

Like a net, the head catches and compresses all impressions. Within its confines lies the final compacted material gathered in from experience, from the senses, from the circling flows of thought, and from the processing of ideas. The net is drawn tight, squeezing all this together within the brain and the nervous system, until one impression can no longer be distinguished from another. From this 'head' – and is it just the skull and its contents, or is it something more? – new impulses arise, darting outwards to reconnect with the crystalline, gossamer-fine network of life. New relationships are formed, new impressions received.

COMMENTARY

In the Kabbalah, the head is an important image. The Tree of Life itself can be depicted as a sacred head. The divine dew, which fertilizes the garden below, is distilled from it. The Great Head is bearded, and each hair acts as a channel for divine energy to flow between the source of creation and living beings. The human head is also a miraculously wrought device, including the brain and neural pathways, the mouth, eyes, ears and nose, and all that they can do. But it is also more than human: it is a version of the cosmic blueprint. Kabbalah shows how the form of every human being is modelled on the divine.

The oracle talks about how we condense all the information that we receive. We also receive and transmit impressions, in the same way that we take an in- and out-breath. We cannot hold on to every thought, every memory because they have to be distilled; sometimes all we are left with is an evocative residue of memory, in which all the ingredients are combined into one wordless substance. Our impressions and memories form a kind of food which sustains us. People who lose their memory are in a terrible situation and no longer know who they are. Even unpleasant memories help to form our sense of identity, and spur us on to new activity.

This is a complex card because there are so many layers of activity concerned with the head, face and brain. In Kabbalah, the forehead is known as the place of grace and mercy.

INTERPRETATIONS

Life tasks: *You need to think something through rather carefully. Take notice of what people say, but use your own reasoning. Keep your senses extended; you will need to select from all the information that is presented to you, but if you close the doors too early, you may miss something.*

Possible meanings: *A debate. Work which challenges your mental faculties. An issue with your boss, or an offer to take up new leadership. A connection that you must make with something outside your normal sphere. An intellectual puzzle.*

THE CARDS

The Sleeper שנת

Wheel 2
Suit: EARTH
COMPANION CARDS:
*The Drunkard, Thirst,
The Uprooted*

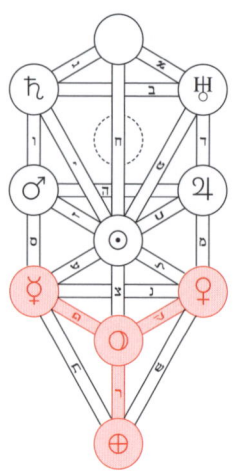

ORACLE
The sleeper finds his way through dreams in which all of life is enacted. Here, things that have been and things that might have been face each other, then they fade as the sleeper realizes that he is asleep, and awakes.

COMMENTARY
The changing experience of dreaming, sleeping and waking provides one of the most fascinating patterns in our lives. From earliest recorded history, dreams have been considered significant. They create awe, wonder and fear in the human heart, and some seem more real than waking life. Through dreams we may catch glimpses of the future, or dream of times long ago before we were born. Although dreams are usually very personal, sometimes those barriers are washed away too, and people may even share dreams. Knowledge may come through dreams; when all our daytime cares and preconceptions are left behind, we can be receptive to the knowledge that lies beyond our limited world, and the voices which speak of it. We should listen to the words of our dreams, and by experience learn which should be discarded as floating fancy, and which are resonant with meaning.

Kabbalah describes each level of existence like the layers and folds of a walnut: 'The whole world is organized on this principle, from the primary mystic centre to the very outermost of all the layers. All are coverings, the one to the other, brain within brain, spirit inside of spirit, shell within shell.' When we know we are sleeping, we usually wake – though sometimes we can continue 'awake' within a dream. We wake to another reality. Many traditions teach that death is a waking from life to yet another reality beyond that.

We are also told that it is the greatest spiritual challenge in life for us to wake up. A person can live on 'automatic', feeding on impressions and emotions as well as on physical food, and simply responding to those changing stimuli. Or he or she can wake up to the birthright of full consciousness, act from real will and take responsibility for his or her actions. The oracle hints at this possibility; within every situation, however deep the sleep, there is that crack through which light appears, and this is our prompt to wake up.

INTERPRETATIONS

Life tasks: *Something inside you is still asleep. Maybe this is a wake-up call. It is your choice, of course, to go on sleeping, but if this is the choice that you make, then you are ignoring the possibilities that lie in front of you. You will no longer be innocent of this.*

Possible meanings: *Unfulfilled potential. Laziness. A period of dormancy. A choice to keep quiet, rather than to act. Retreating into yourself. Someone who will not listen or who cannot be roused.*

THE CARDS

The Drunkard שתנ

Wheel 2
Suit: WATER
COMPANION CARDS:
*The Sleeper, Thirst,
The Uprooted*

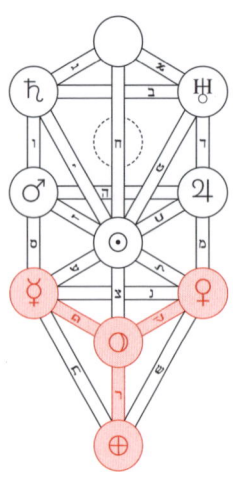

ORACLE

The sweet sensation of memory can be repeated until its impression becomes weak and wasted: memory requires the freshness of the present moment to remain clear. True remembering is not the vain bubbling, mumbling search for a name lost in the days of youthfulness. The glass ought not to be lifted to ghostly images, for they are contaminated, and stink like a drunkard's urine.

COMMENTARY

All desires which arise tend to be circulated over and over again. Here, in the card ruled by the element of water, this flow is intensified. The oracle shows us that we try to repeat our experiences: if one glass of wine is pleasant, so will the next one be, and the next. But gradually, the pleasantness wears off. The sensation that we crave cannot be found any more, though we are still tempted to carry on in the hope that it will return. And this relates not only to physical sensation, but also to what we consume internally – our memories, our desires, the replay of quarrels and triumphs, of romantic encounters and frightening experiences. We recycle these, either to try and enjoy the experiences again, or in the hope of numbing their unpleasant effects. A review of yesterday's unhappy experiences blinds us to the beauty that surrounds us today. We each have our fantasies too, and may spend hours trying to dream them into being. A person can become drunk on memory, fantasies and desires.

But is this drunken indulgence entirely pointless? Kabbalah teaches the principle of balance, but a balance that can be attained only by including extremes and by bringing them into harmony, not by outright rejection. You may experience a build-up of pain, of longing, of joy, which has to be assimilated. Sometimes you need to relieve pressure, and drunkenness is a time-honoured way of doing this, whether it is through a night on the town with your friends or an internal, self-indulgent orgy of sentiment. The way of abstention can lead to far worse events. If you can monitor your own 'flow', and handle its needs with as little destructive output as possible, you are doing well. Even if others don't understand the way you deal with it, you know how to regulate and tune the system.

INTERPRETATIONS

Life tasks: *Take note of your flow of energy. Is it caught up in a whirlpool, going round and round to no good effect? How could you channel it better? Check your outpourings of feelings and responses – are they useful? Only you can truly answer this, and make the changes necessary.*

Possible meanings: *A wasteful output. Someone not to be trusted. A good clear-out. Self-indulgence. Repeating patterns in a project or relationship which are not useful. An excessive reaction. An emotional storm which will pass.*

THE CARDS

Thirst

נשת

Wheel 2
Suit: FIRE
COMPANION CARDS:
The Sleeper, The Drunkard, The Uprooted

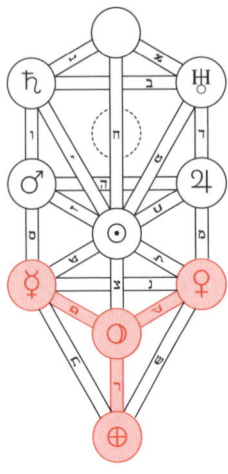

ORACLE

To be dry and parched and to long for water ... To have nearly died, and still to yearn for life ... Thirst is the drive which puts new life into the seedling, but new life cannot be put into the old. Old life cares not for sustenance, but only for memories.

COMMENTARY

Have you seen a newborn baby racked by crying? Its whole body is shaken by the sound, which is created by a ferocious energy. Every day, the baby suffers in this way, primarily from hunger and thirst, and these drives are translated into a convulsive sound more powerful than the baby itself. But this noise is necessary, because the baby has to alert its mother to its needs. It must send out a signal as disruptive as a fire alarm. The quiet baby is in real danger, and every mother knows that a listless baby is likely to be unwell.

Our inner drives still go on making us suffer in adult life, though maybe not so obviously. Some hold the view that these drives can be reduced down to primary survival drives, such as the need for sex and food, whereas others concede that they are more complex, and include drives for power, creativity and a religious imperative. But the yearning for life, which the oracle mentions, is the fundamental urge that keeps us going. We cannot do without it, and although it can cause discomfort, it is what gets us through illnesses, and back on top of life again. It is the kind of optimism that causes us to rush foolishly and headlong into yet another project or relationship. And it is also what stirs us from a deep sleep when a baby cries, because we recognize that intense need in another human being, and will try to satisfy it if we can.

Beware the person who seems to have no appetite for life. Even the most spiritually advanced have their hobbies and their distinctive preferences. And although the oracle implies that old age and thirst for new experience do not go together, this is only true in a general sense. The old person who enjoys small everyday pleasures and who is keen to hear news from the world outside is still living with appetite. But as desire fails, so life dwindles.

INTERPRETATIONS

Life tasks: *What are you thirsty for? Can you acknowledge it, and liberate that urge? Perhaps convention or even your view of yourself is holding you back. We owe allegiance to life, and must allow its imperatives to speak within us, whether we act on them or not.*

Possible meanings: *A powerful desire. An urgent need. Something in danger of dying off for lack of attention. A demanding person. A drive that cannot be satisfied.*

The Uprooted

נתש

Wheel 2
Suit: AIR
COMPANION CARDS:
The Sleeper,
The Drunkard, Thirst

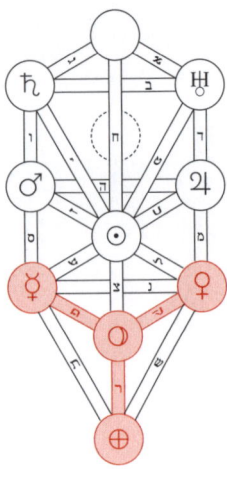

ORACLE

The uprooted has been torn from its life source, as a sapling is torn from the earth. It is wrenched away from what is familiar, and thrust into a new environment. The uprooter of life is experience, which negates previous expectations and offers a new kingdom in which to live.

COMMENTARY

To be uprooted sounds drastic, even disastrous. But the oracle reveals, surprisingly, that it is in fact a natural part of existence. We are in a constant process of being uprooted, if we open ourselves to new experience. And this new experience opens out wider horizons for us. There is a conditional 'if' here though, because it is sometimes easier to block off experience, than to allow it to uproot our cherished views. It is very often hard to open yourself completely to the new. Are you listening to a foreign language? Meeting a person for the first time? Visiting a new country? The chances are that you will look for something familiar in the new, and compare it to something or someone similar that you are acquainted with. We try to accommodate new impressions within our existing framework, and the older we get, the more we assume that our views are complete.

Kabbalah teaches that each seeker on the path must be reborn as a little child. Perhaps this is because a very young child is receptive to new experience and does not hold fixed views. In every moment, there is something new to see – if we allow our eyes to do the looking.

Society both loves and fears the uprooted person. The pedlar, the minstrel, the gypsy and the wandering monk have all been considered both as a rich resource and as a threat to settled civilization. They appear to undermine established values, and do not necessarily share the culture of the communities that they pass through. But they are loved too for the treasures that they bring – their music, their tales, their goods, their teachings, and for their exotic way of life. They stir a desire in people to roam and to see the wonders of the world for themselves. For most people it is enough to touch that desire and then be thankful for their own settled place in life. Some, though, will answer the call and leave their old life behind, learning to live from day to day and experiencing whatever comes their way.

INTERPRETATIONS

Life tasks: *A major change could be coming your way. Be ready to let go of what is outdated, of what you don't need any more. Don't be afraid: there will be new soil for your roots to grow in in due course.*

Possible meanings: *A radical change. A sudden upset, overthrowing existing plans. Travel, roaming, and being on the move. Moving house. An unreliable person. Openness to new experience.*

The Actor

לעשת

Wheel 3
Suit: EARTH

COMPANION CARDS:
The Coward, The Observer, The Moment

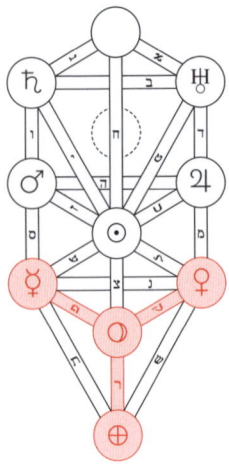

ORACLE

The actor makes you believe. He creates and performs all the tragedies and absurdities of life while you sit and stare. He evokes, he compels, he manipulates situations; he presses and squeezes, and makes dull things appear shiny. Then, when he stops, he points accusingly at you, demanding that you think and that you reconsider. He knows how you are: all the time that he has been acting, you have been growing fat in complacency.

COMMENTARY

The actor is rooted in the personal world, but can touch upon a higher source, bringing it to life before our eyes in flashes of brilliance. He leaves us wide-eyed when he paints our everyday world with magic and glamour. Acting is truth and illusion bound up together. How else do you tell a story of something that is beyond our normal understanding? How else do you make a channel for higher grace to flow through into our everyday world? All this is done by ritual and role-playing. Those who only have eyes for the literal reject ritual and role-playing as meaningless forms. But the symbols used are carefully constructed – a crown to signify the supreme being, a sword for the power of judgement, and a filled cup for the presence of mercy. Our worst despair as human beings comes when we feel cut off from anything greater than ourselves. But we have the chance to bridge that gap. As the Zohar, the mystical book of Kabbalistic writings, says: 'It is thus the yearning from below which brings about the completion above'.

Acting is a great responsibility, spanning two worlds with the medium which connects them always shifting; it is glamorous and iridescent, but also insubstantial. Historically, actors were often despised. They worked on the fringes of society and were rejected by society's more self-satisfied, conventional citizens, even if these people couldn't keep away from the lure of the performance. Actors dress up a truth which can sometimes be painful to acknowledge. They take responsibility for what we are afraid to do for ourselves.

INTERPRETATIONS

Life tasks: *Are you really doing something, or only pretending? You may be in a temporary situation, balancing two different demands or realities. It isn't healthy for everyone to live on the shifting sands, so work out whether you can cope with this, or if it is time to opt for one or the other. Remember that if you continue to balance and juggle, people may call you a chameleon and think you are not serious. They may be wrong, of course.*

Possible meanings: *Being called on to play a particular role. A temporary job or project. Someone who is not to be relied on, although they may have much of interest to communicate. Rumours, gossip. Performance, theatre. A drama in your life.*

The Coward

לשתע

Wheel 3
Suit: WATER
COMPANION CARDS:
The Actor, The Observer, The Moment

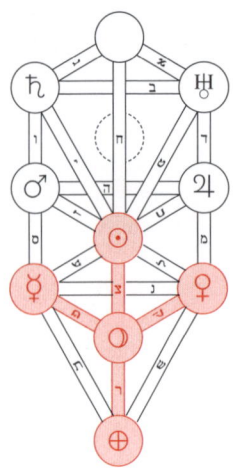

ORACLE
Freeing yourself from the impingements of all forms, while still registering their impressions, is to live. Remembering all the names and consequences that echo and perpetuate themselves in life, is to experience. Studying all your inner responses, and drawing your conclusions with integrity, is to know. But experience without knowledge is cowardly and incestuous.

COMMENTARY
The person who runs away from a situation and acknowledges that he or she is frightened, is not a coward. The person who makes up an excuse for running away is a coward. If you know what you are doing, but reject that knowledge, that is cowardice. So what the oracle is talking about here is escaping from responsibility. The coward really does have something in common with the actor, because we all have that edge of social cowardice, when we make up and act out little lies to explain our omissions and failures. We turn the truth around to make it seem as though we are the passive victims of circumstance. We create roles to sustain our image as worthy, reliable, considerate people, and we are skilled at acting

out these roles. Indeed, the person who bluntly says, 'I didn't feel like doing it,' creates a nervous ripple around the room. Others may be shocked and hurt to be presented with such a bald statement of disinclination.

So are cowards necessary? Maybe. It depends if you yourself believe the lies you tell, because ignoring knowledge is here pointed out as the hallmark of the coward. But if you know you are blurring those borders between truth and illusion, and you can accept any consequences that may follow, then you are not a coward. If you can speak whatever truth is necessary, you can play with the rest as you think appropriate for the situation. Consider the needs of others, and try to sense what truth must be revealed or concealed. This is the beginning of real conscience. What we learn from our parents and our religion are guidelines, but true morality comes from within. Sometimes, even hiding behind the rules we have been taught can be cowardice.

INTERPRETATIONS

Life tasks: *Are you living with a lie? Ask yourself what it is, and if it is holding you back. Is there something that you need to tackle? What would be the very worst that could happen if you abandon that lie or take on that need? If you can face that worst-case scenario, then you have nothing else to fear.*

Possible meanings: *A betrayal, or a person who acts as a traitor. Lies. An area of life in which you are falling short or selling yourself short. Fear of the unknown. Having the wisdom to hold back rather than rushing in recklessly.*

The Observer

לשעת

Wheel 3
Suit: FIRE
COMPANION CARDS:
*The Actor, The Coward,
The Moment*

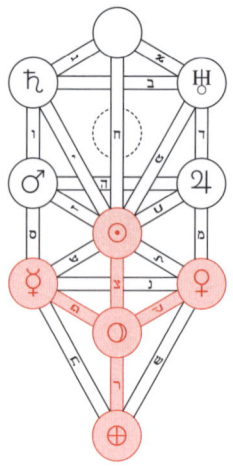

ORACLE

The glance proceeds out of the eye and down on to the earth. And for a little while, the earth is stilled. Steadily all is noticed, even the silent flickering and the secret properties of the eye. Then the earth appears to move, and for a moment the eye looks inward.

COMMENTARY

Observation plays a fundamental part in all kinds of training. The airline pilot, the scientist, the nurse, the artist, the naturalist, the performer all have to be observant. The same goes for inner work, such as learning the practice of meditation or studying the Tree of Life. You learn to note all the slight changes and responses, and you must be on the look-out for anything unusual. From observation, you can gather material, food for your research or your writing, findings for your prescription or prognosis. Observation helps to purify false impressions and to hone our energies.

Observation is part of a cycle, so that we turn to inward reflection after focusing on external data. Sometimes, as we pass over the threshold between inner and outer, we can catch glimpses of strange, half-hidden phenomena, such as the flow of images and thoughts that float on the edge of consciousness, or, as the oracle suggests, the kind of visual phenomena that occur when we see specks of light or colour, or even the pattern of blood vessels in the eye itself.

There are some really significant thresholds where we can gain extraordinary knowledge as the attention moves between outward and inward, or in reverse: the borders between sleeping and waking, for instance. If you are seeking hidden knowledge, seek out such known borders and explore them. There are all kinds of examples, both physical and invisible: borders between countries, the cusp between astrological signs, the moment of birth, the passage between life and death, the changeover from thought to feeling. Observation is the key to these thresholds, because usually we pass over without recognizing what happens there. 'Liminal' places are acknowledged and honoured in human ritual, and rites of passage often accompany transitions of age, as from childhood to puberty for example. But no one should linger on the border forever.

INTERPRETATIONS

Life tasks: *You may be entering a phase when you can only observe attentively; you have done what you can, and now you must wait for the results. Don't drift off to sleep. Noting your own accurate impressions will be very valuable in the times to come. You can gather material, even if you can't yet do anything with it.*

Possible meanings: *The chance to view something of great interest. An eagle-eyed observer. Surveillance. Spying. Keeping an eye on someone or something. Making a report. An inspection.*

The Moment

של עת

Wheel 3
Suit: AIR

COMPANION CARDS:
The Actor, The Coward, The Observer

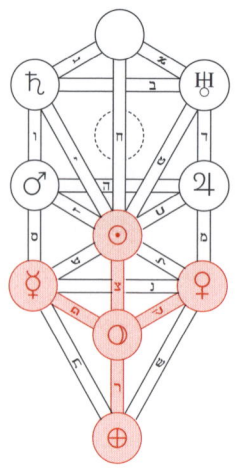

ORACLE

It is the time to sing. It is the time in which all curses are fulfilled. It is the time to do what must be done. But we can lose that moment and its content. We beg for it to be repeated, and then, if we can turn the wheel and reclaim it, we believe ourselves to be in secure possession of it. Hugging its forms and names to ourselves, we look up – and find that knowledge has fled, and the precious experience has vanished like the morning mist.

COMMENTARY

We would like to think of the moment as a discrete little piece of time, the smallest that we can recognize. But a 'moment' suggests not so much a fixed measure of time as the shortest attention span that we can register. To live in the moment therefore suggests living with attention.

This is hard, though not impossible. Like all the cards in this set, the moment suggests keeping a balance in a slippery situation. We can either be 'asleep' and miss it, or else we can analyze what we have just experienced, and then realize that the experience itself has fled. No one can live without planning, or indeed without using memory, even if it means slipping out of the moment. But there is a point of alertness, where the eagle is poised on its high perch, aware of all that is within its range of vision and ready to focus on anything of significance. The ideal is not to discard all knowledge of past and future, but to let it be present within our general consciousness. We can trust the mind to pick up what is of importance and to register anything within that field of attention which we need to examine more closely. In meditation, we go further and gently release even those moments of interest that appear. The watching eagle here never swoops for the kill.

As the oracle says, each moment brings its own quality of joy, dread or action. This is the normal colouring of human life, which is always in a state of change. Each moment has its mood and its imperative. But it may be up to us whether we act on that imperative, or not.

INTERPRETATIONS

Life tasks: *Living with the present rather than trying to project too far into the future is important to you now. You also need to pay close attention to what arises, because some kind of opportunity will come up which you will miss if you're not careful.*

Possible meanings: *A brief spell of time. An imminent event. A chance not to be missed. A situation which is changing from moment to moment. A pattern of flux. Living on the edge, with excitement and uncertainty.*

THE CARDS

The Locksmith נעל

Wheel 4
Suit: EARTH
COMPANION CARDS:
*The Eater, The Witness,
The Wanderer*

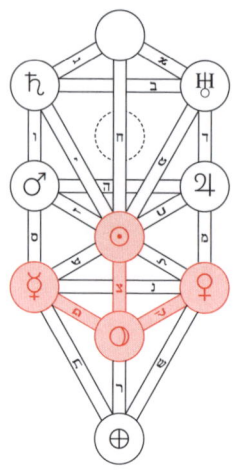

ORACLE
The locksmith is a cautious man, making his living from a cautious trade. He builds devices to lock and bind precious golden objects which yearn for the fresh and cheering rays of daylight. He thinks to keep and have forever, but locks prefer to remain closed and keyholes become smaller with disuse.

COMMENTARY
Every organization has someone who guards its resources so closely that it is almost impossible to get at them. Supplies are released with painful slowness and doors unlocked grudgingly. It seems an unnecessary hindrance, but it brings security, and guards against waste. It is also a display of respect for what has been created, bought, given or wrought. The role of the locksmith, like others in this set, is not satisfactory if you see it as an absolute. The protector who has no counterbalance will end up by impounding everything of value and refusing access to all. Locks become stiffer and, over time, people forget what lies behind closed doors. But in the body of an organization, a family or a community, the different roles play off against each other. The locksmith will be challenged by those who want to use those

protected resources. Maybe without the locksmith, they would run to extravagance and then complain that there is nothing left to use.

Hiders and keepers over the centuries have provided wonderful discoveries for later generations – a pot of gold is dug up in a ploughed field; a bag of jewels found hidden in a chimney. The misguided belief that valuables could be made safe in this way enriches us in extraordinary ways. There is not only unexpected wealth for the finder, but perhaps a story to be unlocked and fresh light shed on history.

Think about what you lock up: it may pass out of your hands altogether and into the earth's slow cycle of concealment and revelation.

INTERPRETATIONS

Life tasks: *You cannot achieve utter security. You can take reasonable precautions to protect, but beyond that you will only create the opposite effect, putting something out of your reach altogether. It may spoil and tarnish if it is never used. Relationships are the same; we can never be completely certain of another person, and we have to grant them the freedom to make their own choices. By all means work for stability, look after your possessions and your relationships with love and care, but in the end you are only the caretaker, not the jailer.*

Possible meanings: *A guard or caretaker. Locks, codes and protective mechanisms. Caution. Check your boundaries and your security measures. Specialist help is useful, but set your own limits on it. Something is locked up that should be released. Overprotectiveness. The challenge of passing through a locked door.*

The Eater

נלע

Wheel 4
Suit: WATER
COMPANION CARDS:
The Locksmith, The Witness, The Wanderer

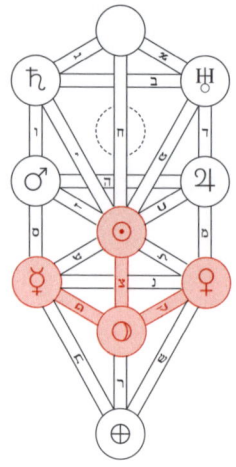

ORACLE

The eater gobbled all his food down, gulping and hiccupping, and frantically explaining that he must eat all he could, for there might not be any more tomorrow. He ate and he ate, and the more he ate, the less it seemed that he could taste anything. He blamed the food and accused it of having less flavour and goodness than it used to have. Specks and crumbs of food flew everywhere and all the onlookers were disgusted by his gluttony. But under his chair, ran a little mouse in great excitement. It found one of these dropped morsels and quietly thanked heaven for it.

COMMENTARY

Sometimes we discover little morsels of luck dropped at our feet by providence. Imagine, if you will, the workings of heaven producing an excess of benevolence and scattering it around carelessly. Kabbalah reveals that there is a perpetual flow between the higher and lower worlds. The cup of mercy is always refilled and it overflows into our lives, though we can't always glimpse its source. What is luck? Not all languages and cultures recognize the idea. Some attribute it to the gods, and say that their moods cause our good or bad fortune. Others see it as reward or punishment for our own actions. Was the mouse merely lucky? Or was she able to be in the right place through her own well-focused will? Perhaps she was an extremely deserving mouse. At any rate, she had the sense to be grateful for her reward. Think about your own lucky breaks and what prompted them.

Then there is the eater: the greedy person too has a role to play in processing the forces of life. Extravagance and waste are also part of the natural cycles. Watch how horses snort at fresh green grass, greedily snatching a mouthful here and there. Or see how children splash water, and throw handfuls of sand or snow in an ecstasy of plenty.

Perhaps you don't want to be like the eater, consuming more and more for less reward. That is another matter entirely. The presence of Essence on this card means that there is an element of choice in how we shape our drives and desires.

INTERPRETATIONS

Life tasks: *If you have plenty, consider how you can share this with others. If you have excessive habits of consumption, think how best to temper them. But remember that total abstinence isn't always the best way. Keep the flow going, keep generosity circulating, and you will not suffer from loss of appetite.*

Possible meanings: *Extravagance and excess. A greedy person. Someone who is taking too much. A project that will consume too much money or resources. Appetites and desires. An over-enthusiastic approach. Carelessness. Surplus.*

THE CARDS

The Witness

לענ

Wheel 4
Suit: FIRE

COMPANION CARDS:
The Locksmith, The Eater, The Wanderer

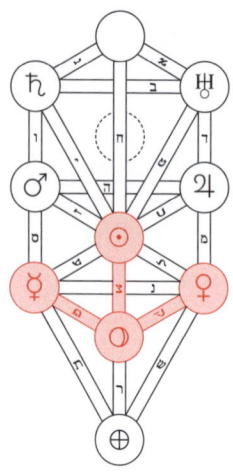

ORACLE

The witness who testifies honestly is living with the law. The person who utters a prayer sincerely is living with God. When the One speaks to the Other, from the truth of his or her own being, a response is called forth. The flame below is lit and conjoins for a while with the fire above. The response expands and the answer is louder than the question. But witnesses who are eager to shout the truth too loudly and too often may drown out the answer, because their ears are too full of their own noise.

COMMENTARY

The flame of truth permeates this card. This is the person who honestly wants to act in accordance with justice. But he or she is also too keen to promote this truth, believing it to be the only one. It does take courage to be a witness. It takes belief in oneself to stand up in front of a court of law or to speak out in the face of hostile opposition. Many people don't want to risk confrontation, so we should appreciate the person who is not afraid to speak out, even though that bluntness may sometimes be inappropriate, and the testimony often limited.

In the realm of prayer, the situation is rather different. Here, a sense of discrimination must prevail. If a person is in extreme anguish, then his or her cry of anguish is a naked prayer. But where we have a choice to pray, then we should think carefully about what we are asking for. Are we trying to gratify our own desires and force through results that we, with our limited vision, think are best? Or are we really submitting a petition and waiting for the response according to divine will?

We can choose to behave according to our personal dictates, which means speaking out automatically. Or we can question those presumptions and bring our testimony as witnesses only where it will be most effective. Each person has a unique voice. Each voice is of value. Each heart is warmed by its own inner truth.

INTERPRETATIONS

Life tasks: *Uncover the flame of truth in your heart. Be ready to speak out, even if you are opposed, and even if you are not believed. Truth does speak to truth, and there will be a response, even if you cannot detect it immediately. Acknowledge the viewpoint of others, though: yours is not the only one. What are you witnessing? Of what will your life have spoken? Think about your contribution, not only today, but what it will mean after you are dead.*

Possible meanings: *Outspokenness. A court case. The need to testify the truth. Confession. The opinion of others. Your personal contribution. A voice that cannot be ignored.*

THE CARDS

The Wanderer

לנע

Wheel 4
Suit: AIR

COMPANION CARDS:
*The Locksmith,
The Eater, The Witness*

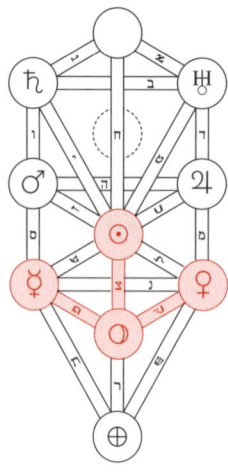

ORACLE
Hither and thither goes the wanderer. Over great mountains high with uncertainty, across seas deep with possibility, to shores of endless variety. And as he shakes the dust of one place from his boots, so even the bones of the dead tremble. For the echo of his foot induces endless motion that reverberates and quivers like the reflection of the moon upon a startled pond.

COMMENTARY
The image of the wanderer has gripped the imagination throughout history. In classical myth, Hermes is the archetypal traveller and messenger, the trickster and guide, patron of the crossroads and helper of lost souls. The person who is an experienced wanderer may be able to help others who have lost their way.

The meditator, too, is a wanderer, setting out on an inner journey to visit the hidden places of the mind. A wanderer has to have flexibility, and must be able to survive the lack of a permanent home. Where is your true home, after all?

In Greek myth, Odysseus and Penelope were both wanderers. His was the external journey over many lands and seas, hers the internal one pictured in the tapestry that she wove patiently while she waited for him to return. Her shuttle and loom worked rhythmically, steadily, to produce a pattern from out of apparently random colours and threads of wool. Only at the end of any journey is the pattern complete.

There has to be purpose to the wandering: it is not necessarily one goal or destination. Wandering to acquire knowledge also has true purpose, but you may not know exactly where it will take you. The heroes of fairy tales often set out with the simple aim of seeking their fortune, and from that many adventures, both marvellous and terrible, arose.

Wanderers carry the pollen of one place to another on their boots, cross-fertilizing, just as troubadours carried stories and songs to those they visited in different cities. Wanderers, too, may create disturbance where they tread, because their arrival will inevitably change things for others. It is impossible to create permanent barriers – the wanderer will always find a way of crossing them.

INTERPRETATIONS

Life tasks: *You are on the move, but do you know why? Do you have some real purpose, even if you cannot put it into words? Or are you wandering aimlessly because you are afraid to settle down? Search your heart for the answer. Only you can know the truth of this; some people fear wanderers, others envy them, but no one else but you understands where you are going or why.*

Possible meanings: *Travel. Freelance work. Living without a permanent base for home or work. A transient relationship. An inner journey, taking you into unexplored territory. Contact with other cultures.*

The Skeleton

צלע פקן

Wheel 5
Suit: EARTH
COMPANION CARDS:
The Sluggard,
The Dancer, The Advisor

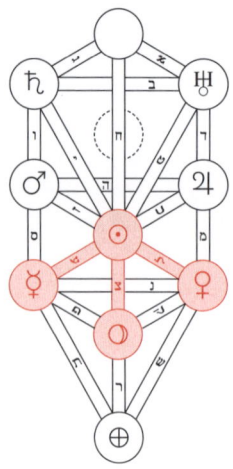

ORACLE

Without skin, muscle, sinews and tissue, the skeleton hangs limply. Without this covering, it is neither able to protect the organs of the body nor enclose them. But without a skeleton, nothing can stand.

COMMENTARY

The earth cards are often to do with the form of things. We never see our own skeleton, unless it is on scans or x-rays, yet the skeleton is the vital structure that dictates the form of our bodies. Some strict meditation practices require the monk or meditator to contemplate their own skeleton. Traces of this are found in general culture, when the bones of the skeleton rattle at Halloween, or jerk about in the macabre Dance of Death. Skeletons make us giggle – fearfully – because they are both comic and a sharp reminder of our own mortality. Why are they comic? It is said that humour arises out of incongruity. Who could believe that such an attractive, softly-skinned, silver-tongued human being could have such a mawkish assemblage of bleached bones inside? What are those huge dark holes in the skull? Why does the jaw hang slackly and the teeth look like those of a predatory animal?

Skeletons are not for the faint-hearted, and so we make jokes out of them.

To acquire the knowledge that is possible here, you have to absorb this deep and terrifying sense of our own form, for which the skeleton is both a symbol and an inner reality. The clothing of flesh and hair, the fluidity of movement and the quick responses of brain and nervous system are admired and worshipped. But they are all given shape by the skeleton.

The skeleton may also stand for our genetic inheritance, which often we prefer to turn away from, imagining ourselves to be entirely self-motivated beings. It can also represent the sheer physicality of being, which even the most illuminated mystic cannot do without. It signifies, too, the form of our lives, the habits which give day-to-day structure, and the patterns of action and reaction which give us the sense of consistency. Yes, the skeleton can be a terrifying image to reflect upon.

INTERPRETATIONS

Life tasks: *Don't seek for novelty when you should be looking at the fundamental framework of your life. You may need to strengthen that structure. Just as a weakness in one bone can cause a fracture, and bring the whole body tumbling down, so any neglected area of your basic set-up can likewise bring everything to a halt. The most mundane aspects of life also need their share of care and attention.*

Possible meanings: *Routine work. A call to look at the hidden form of things, not just at appearances. Attention to basics. A naked form or framework that must be clothed and cherished.*

The Sluggard

פנק עצל

Wheel 5
Suit: WATER
COMPANION CARDS:
*The Skeleton,
The Dancer, The Advisor*

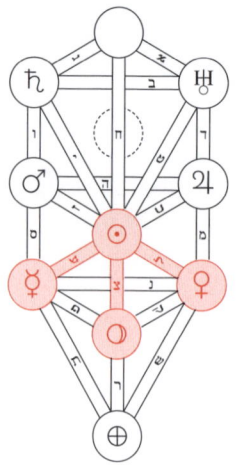

ORACLE

All that there is to be known cannot be known unless there is the desire to know. All that there is to be seen cannot be seen unless it is looked for. All that there is to be found cannot be found unless a search is begun to find it.

COMMENTARY

When a person acquires maturity and self-knowledge, he or she is inclined to be idle. The water cards in these first wheels tend, in any case, to be rather lazy, and to indulge in the comfortable flow of events instead of taking initiative. In the later wheels, the water oracles are roused and stirred by movement. But here it is tempting to bask in the golden solar light at the centre, and to imagine that now one has grasped everything essential about life.

In the cycle of life much of childhood is spent grappling with our physical body and senses. Adolescence develops and painfully explores the personality. The first part of adult life is concerned with seeking out the inner core of life, the essence. If it is found, the mature adult reaches a point of stability, and the inclination to go no further is strong. Complacency can set in, but this is not, in fact, the end of the story, and someone trapped by this self-satisfaction can have less to give than a keen novice or newcomer.

In Kabbalah, the first level of Tiferet (Essence) is symbolized by a newly born child. But just as our physical body develops from infancy to adulthood, so the golden youth has to leave childhood behind to grow into a strong adult and finally into a majestic king or queen. Thus the myth is completed and a human being develops full potential, partaking both of material and divine worlds.

The Sluggard is not so much a lazy person, as one who refuses to acknowledge there is further to go. It is someone who takes their store of knowledge and says 'This is all.' It is someone who reviews their life experience and says 'It's in my memory now – no need to look further.' When people give up on the quest, life will eventually give up on them, for nothing can ever stay completely static.

INTERPRETATIONS

Life tasks: *Don't get trapped by inertia. You have achieved much already, but you need to turn your face to the future, rather than just being satisfied with the past. The situation you are in may need a very active shake-up, and you will have to arouse any others who are also involved.*

Possible meanings: *Laziness. A period of rest or inactivity. An area of life that is blocked or silted up. Someone who obstructs your way from habit or inertia. A delay. Lack of energy or physical debility.*

The Dancer

עלצ נקף

Wheel 5
Suit: FIRE

COMPANION CARDS:
The Skeleton, The Sluggard, The Advisor

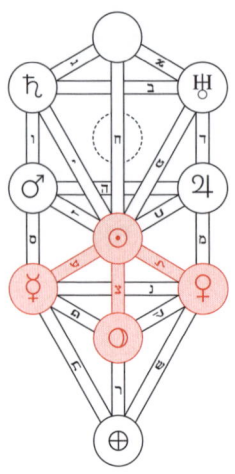

ORACLE

The dancer begins to make the steps that will form a circle. She moves here and there, with lightness and rhythm; she dances both towards you and retreats away from you. But as she moves away, so she moves towards herself. She gazes at the fire in the glowing embers, studying its light and heat and discovering how closely she may approach it in safety. When she knows, then, with arms outstretched she may complete the circle gloriously. She may look both inwards and outwards, without impairing the knowledge that she cherishes.

COMMENTARY

Like most fire cards, this one is very active; as suggested in the description of this wheel, the cards in this set represent either inertia or movement. Fire always seeks excitement and fuel for its flames. The dancer is never at rest for long. She is stirred by the song of the birds at dawn, and as evening comes she dances to celebrate the last glimmer of daylight. For her, movement creates more energy, and the dance itself is life, creating more life. However, the dancer must be disciplined. There is no beauty in the dance without balance and poise. The true dancer does not dance simply to rid herself of surplus energy, but in answer to a question. A true dance reflects both question and answer, and even after the answer, there is a question mark.

When you discover your own real inner energy, it is an awesome moment. Many people are frightened of this and call it magic, possession or the evil influence of others. Why? Simply because it is so powerful, and yet in one sense so impersonal. What relation can it possibly have to the nice, well-socialized person that you know you are?

The dancer has the courage to take on that question too, and become acquainted with that power. She discovers that it will not burn her, if she approaches it correctly. She celebrates its light with joy, dancing in the circle that has been the mystic symbol of the sun's wheel since time began. Does she dance for herself, for the sun or for the onlooker? Maybe for all three – but her attention must be on the movement of the dance itself.

INTERPRETATIONS

Life tasks: *It is time to celebrate that which you have. Life itself is a cause for celebration, but you also have much to rejoice in your own circumstances. The act of celebration will open the door to new experience and activities. You can give expression to your energy and joy, but use your energy skilfully.*

Possible meanings: *A cause for joy. Plenty of activity and movement. Short journeys to and fro. Celebration, a party. Physical discipline and training. Sports, dance. Giving something a light but skilful touch.*

The Advisor

נפק לעץ

Wheel 5
Suit: AIR

COMPANION CARDS:
The Skeleton, The Sluggard, The Dancer

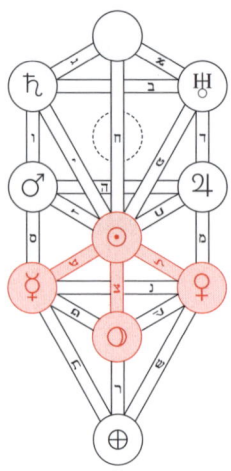

ORACLE

'And the tree issued a promise, and the promise blossomed into a golden flower which adorned the tree. Humming resounded perpetually amongst its shining petals, and when the sun declined, the flower would close, hugging to itself the potent pollen of experience. The tree would then sigh, stretching forth its branches, as its new wood demanded a place in the air.' This the advisor told the neophyte.

COMMENTARY

Now myths begin to arise. The truths that must be related when higher and lower worlds meet cannot be understood in normal terms. Images, symbols and myths must be brought into play. The cards of air are often the storytellers, because they clothe the most delicate of concepts in words and catch our attention with the beauty that they describe. The last air card was the wanderer, and wanderers were often the traditional storytellers of society, bringing news and tales with them from other lands.

Here too begins the world of magic. Magic is the manipulation of images so that they cause an interaction between higher and lower worlds. Even advertising is a form of magic, though a base one. Just as our psychology and our desires can be affected by the manipulation of imagery and sensory input, so if you align yourself with the powers that lie behind the appearance of things, you can bring about change in the visible world, usually by directing your intention through symbols and instruments. Magic discovered, revealed and understood, becomes science. Science rejects the magic that gave it birth, because science then sets about its own work in the world.

Whatever you give birth to will be wrested away from you and other meanings will be imposed on it. Never create unless you are willing to give away your creations. Send them out into the world with integrity and they will find their own mark there.

But you can make a beautiful myth out of what you create. That way, future generations will keep returning to wonder at the golden flower and to smell its fragrance, which no one can adequately describe. They will not be satisfied with the cut-and-dried interpretations that their parents give to things; they will return with yearning to the source.

INTERPRETATIONS

Life tasks: *It may be the moment to become either a pupil or a teacher – or both. The transmission of knowledge is important; if you want to go further, you will need to find someone who can train you adequately. If you have knowledge, then you need to pass it on. But you must find your own ways and means of doing this.*

Possible meanings: *Magical initiation. A period of teaching or of training. Creative work, especially involving myth and story. Advice or consultation. Instructions. A new subject to study.*

THE CARDS

Pandora's Box   מקפסה

Wheel 6
Suit: EARTH
COMPANION CARDS:
Applause, The Edge, The Surgeon

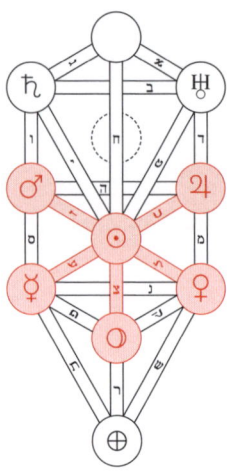

ORACLE
Jupiter gave Pandora, the first mortal woman, a box containing all the blessings of the gods. But when she opened it, all the blessings flew out – all, that is, except Hope, which was at the bottom.

COMMENTARY
Hope leaves the human heart last of all. The world is full of people who are still hoping against hope – that they will find a loved one who is missing, be cured of a terrible disease or even recover their lost fortunes. A belief in miracles springs up, however much science and reason try to dampen it. Many people spend their time and money searching for the one miracle that would restore to them what they have lost. A sane, well-balanced individual may pity them, because they do not listen to common sense. But miracles have been known to happen. Many things whose possibility is denied today will tomorrow prove to be possible after all. And the sanest, most rational person will find that he or she too will cling on to that one shred of hope when in the throes of grief or desperation.

Although Pandora's Box is a Greek myth, the story has been adopted here as a way of interpreting this card, since the Hebrew word taken from around the rim of this wheel means 'box'. This is the kindest version of the Pandora story. The other tells us that the gods made her as a woman to punish mankind, and that her box or vase was filled with afflictions and diseases which spread all over the earth when the box was opened. What is a curse, or a blessing? Can they sometimes be the same thing? It is said 'Be careful what you ask for, in case you get it.'

Anyone who wants to live fully and to develop their potential will inevitably open Pandora's Box at some stage. Folly or natural misfortune will make sure of that. There is loss, but ultimately gain too. Much that is unnecessary will be cleared when this process of opening the box takes place.

INTERPRETATIONS

Life tasks: *The old saying 'Count your blessings' may prove invaluable here. Much of what you relied on may now have deserted you, but look for what is left, because that will be your real hope for the future. Perhaps you still have a choice to open Pandora's Box. If so, consider your options wisely. It may not yet be time to do so or it may be someone else's task. There is no point in stirring up needless trouble.*

Possible meanings: *A shock; a sudden revelation. A situation which is full of prickly problems. A decision whether to act or not. A sign of hope. Being ready to face the consequences of your actions.*

THE CARDS

Applause   ספק מה

Wheel 6
Suit: WATER
COMPANION CARDS:
*Pandora's Box,
The Edge, The Surgeon*

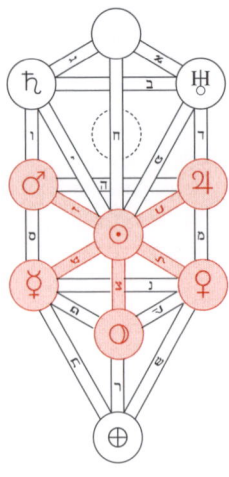

ORACLE

Applause gives recognition and acceptance. It may be given in joy or sadness, but its generosity is a sign that the audience recognizes the possibilities in what they have witnessed and accepts the shortcomings of the performance. Applause arouses, consoles and encourages.

COMMENTARY

Traditions of applause vary in different parts of the world. In the West, the audience applauds and the performers bow to accept this tribute. In some Eastern cultures, the performers salute the audience by applauding too. Applause is usually loud and reverberating. Clapping, shouting, whistling, ululating and stamping are all forms, though to someone who had never heard applause, it could be terrifying to experience. How do you know whether applause is noisy approval or a prelude to collective aggression? This is the pact between performer and audience, where both parties accept that this is the normal conclusion to a performance. Each must trust the other: the audience trusts the performers to give their very best performance – flawed or otherwise – and to bring the performance to a close when appropriate. The performers on their part trust the audience to acknowledge their efforts, so that they may go home whole, not depleted. But every now and then, applause does run out of control, and becomes rioting that ruins concerts, matches and political assemblies. Lives have even been lost through applause.

Living involves interaction with others. We must acknowledge their best efforts, especially if we want the same acknowledgement for ourselves. There should be trust in the right measure of giving and taking, and also a confidence that each party will round off the transaction properly. An open-ended transaction drains away energy. Give generously through applause, because you never know when it will be your turn to face the public with a dry mouth and racing heart.

Although applause is chiefly associated with performance, we look for it in many situations in life, for work well done or a witty remark made. Even a cat relishes applause when it has caught a mouse. If it doesn't win your approval, it has to go out and catch another.

INTERPRETATIONS

Life tasks: *You are seeking recognition. This may hold you back, unless you also give such recognition generously to others. But recognition that you receive for a particular situation will only come your way once – if you try to get it repeated, you may block your own path. When you have received recognition, move on. And do not blame others for a lack of response. Applause can reasonably be expected, but never compelled.*

Possible meanings: *Praise for a job well done. The end of a task. Recognition from others. Conceit. Confirmation or approval from outside sources. Performance. The need for assessment.*

The Edge

סף קמה

Wheel 6
Suit: FIRE

COMPANION CARDS:
*Pandora's Box,
Applause, The Surgeon*

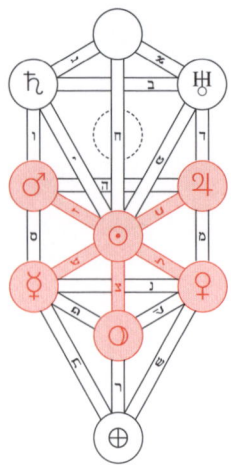

ORACLE

Being on the edge means to rest upon the threshold, to stand upon the verge of maturity, just as the yellowing grains of corn are when poised on the brink of ripeness. Striving to complete the transition, they reach out for the warm rays of the sun, which will penetrate to the heart of the corn grains and give them the life they need. All comes to maturity, sustenance is passed on, old life aids new life to grow.

COMMENTARY

There are those who pass over that threshold, and there are those who dance upon it, aiding others to pass to and fro. Their motto is 'Keep to the edge of the field, and leave the corn for others.' There are those who consume, and those who observe the consumption. Two birds sit in a tree; one eats, and the other watches its mate enjoy the fruits of that tree. In the human psyche there is the one who enjoys and the one who is indifferent, the one who is involved with the affairs of the world, and the other who is detached. The interplay between them marks out much of life's struggle, for both are necessary, and neither can win. They are marked on the Tree of Life by Essence, the centred observer, and Experience, the moving actor.

But each person has their rightful preference of where to look and what to achieve. Do you prefer to aid the growth of others or do you strive to reach your own golden goals? In the last analysis, will you step back and make way for others or will you fight to establish your place in the ranks? Both modes of being demand respect.

Each person too must strike some sort of a balance and make peace in that internal war. The person who always gives way to others does not do them any favours. The person who only promotes their own interests crushes much else that is of value.

In one area you have no choice: the next generation will oust you. If you accept it graciously, you may be able to contribute to it. If you try to hold your position for too long, you will sow the seeds of discord.

INTERPRETATIONS

Life tasks: *This is a point of change, where you can take stock of how far you have come and how far you hope to go. At a time of transition, you may lose the strong sense of your own identity and so you must trust the volition that will take you from one phase to the next.*

Possible meanings: *Everything is finely balanced. A new beginning. Handing over to a successor. Interaction with another generation. A choice. The result is not yet determined, and could go either way.*

The Surgeon

פסה מק

Wheel 6
Suit: AIR
COMPANION CARDS:
*Pandora's Box,
Applause, The Edge*

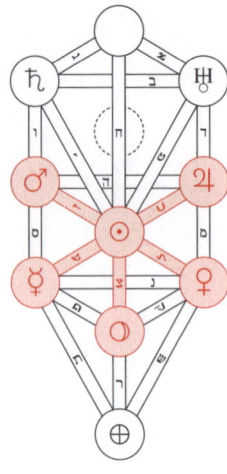

ORACLE
When a person knows more than he needs to know, that knowledge is similar to a malignant tumour, which the surgeon must cut away. The person who has as much as he needs, and more, must start to give that abundance away, before it becomes a sterile possession and starts to fester in dark stagnation.

COMMENTARY
The grim face of this image holds a truth that is more joyful than it at first might appear. What you have, and what you give away, will be replenished. There is a source of never-failing generosity in the universe; it is we ourselves who often block the way to it. Possessions are a temporary retention of the flow of creation in a form useful for our needs. When that usefulness ceases to be relevant, then it is time to let them go.

How can there be too much knowledge? Real knowledge is not retention, because knowledge is like a common pool from which we can all drink. The person who has found the way to knowledge can thus dip into this pool at any time. There is no need to put permanent form on it or to store it greedily.

Accessing knowledge and passing it on keeps our own channels clear and open.

This card represents the element of air because air grants us the ability to observe processes at work and thus to act upon the other elements, especially water. Many of our actions involve the watery flows and handling the chalice whose liquid represents the sacred benevolence of life. A body on which the surgeon operates is not dissimilar to the river, as it is largely composed of water and depends utterly on the reliability of flow - the pumping of blood through the veins. The surgeon aims to restore the promise of life to the patient; the priest provides a means to pass on blessings to his people. Both must act precisely, impersonally and attentively. Personal emotion has no place in ritual, for it is a way of hijacking the operation for yourself, and in surgery this could prove disastrous.

INTERPRETATIONS

Life tasks: *You need to choose what to let go of. Too much of anything, even love, can be a burden if its energy is not fed back into circulation again. You may also be asked to diagnose the problems or blockages in someone else's work or life. Keep their wellbeing in mind, and take away only as much as is necessary.*

Possible meanings: *The need to cut back. Someone that must be cut out of your life – or who cuts you out of theirs. An area of neglect that needs attention. Budgets, streamlined programming. Counselling and consultations to weed out trouble spots. De-cluttering. Medical operation. Job losses. Freedom after unnecessary burdens have been removed.*

The Heart

דמ קפ סוב

Wheel 7
Suit: EARTH
COMPANION CARDS:
The Warrior,
The Victor, The Treasury

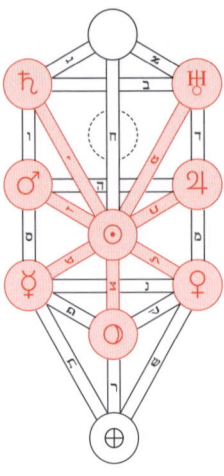

ORACLE

The heart must beat just as the sun must shine. It must continue to turn in its own orbit and propel its energies into other orbits around it. And those energies must attract purpose as the blood attracts oxygen.

COMMENTARY

The heart sees itself as the centre of the body's universe. Each person considers themself to be at the centre of the world. It is almost impossible to function except when that sense of centre exists. The more faculties and powers that fall within the sphere of consciousness, the richer and more blessed that centre feels. It may be ready to claim possession of all that falls within its orbit, because that is in its nature too, just as a parent surrounded by children feels powerful and benevolent. But even when we feel secure at the heart of our world, we have to continue both giving and receiving. The heart must not be self-serving, even though it may be self-important. The parent must not give self-indulgently, but only according the true needs of the child, whatever the age of the child.

Any organization or group of people that has someone functioning as its heart, is a living body. That person helps to focus its interactions and to send new energy coursing through its body. This isn't always the obvious boss; in fact we call the boss 'the head', suggesting someone who thinks and plans for others, not someone who responds and energizes as the heart does. Where there is nobody acting as the heart, there is only an institution, not a living organism. A body with a heart may be authoritarian but it has love, warmth and genuine feeling. It gives a sense of value to its members and they feel part of a whole.

Many of us are used to acting from the head and need to learn how to respond from the heart. This is not simply a case of intellect versus emotion. The heart has its own logic too, which is to promote the well-being of the whole.

INTERPRETATIONS

Life tasks: *You are in a position where you have both responsibility and abundance. Whether that abundance is in money, relationships, work or creativity, you need to keep it alive and enriched with your own energy. Make sure that you can really serve all those people and projects which rely on your input. If any one of them becomes too demanding or dominating, refer to the welfare of the whole to decide how much you really need to give to the individual.*

Possible meanings: *Health and welfare of the body. The heart of the matter. A true connection with someone. Warm feelings. Source of energy. Commitment. A person who has great significance for you. Falling in love.*

The Warrior

קם דב וספ

Wheel 7
Suit: WATER
COMPANION CARDS:
*The Heart, The Victor,
The Treasury*

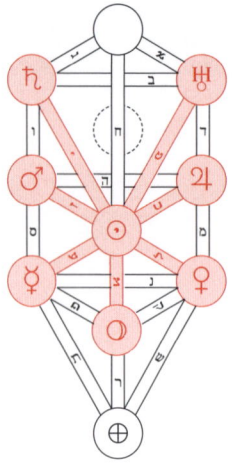

ORACLE
Follow the eye; let the gaze move smoothly, so that it can bear a true image of what it has caught. Then let the hand move with expedition, gliding and sweeping through the air as if invisible, on to the agitated brow of the adversary.

COMMENTARY
At first glance, it seems unusual that the warrior is associated with the element of water. Why not with the energy of fire or with quick-thinking air? Perhaps it is because the world of the warrior is one of fluid change. He or she must pick the right moment for action, interrupting the flow of the enemy's movements with an initiative of his or her own. Those who practise martial arts know that the flow is all-important and that every movement must be smooth, even if it appears to the onlooker as a lightning strike. There is no place for jerky action. As the oracle says, even the way you look around you must be smooth. As a warrior, you must see everything and miss nothing.

Incisiveness comes from understanding fluidity, but not being caught by it. To be a warrior is to have a goal, and whatever stands between the warrior and his goal must be removed. As a warrior, you must employ the decisive stroke that separates useful from redundant, good from bad, healthy from diseased. The gardener is a warrior, lopping off ailing branches, uprooting weeds that threaten to choke the flowers. The cook is a warrior, cutting the fat from the meat and paring the skin from vegetables. The psychologist is a warrior, listening patiently to everything, but cutting through to the core of real meaning. The academic is a warrior, considering all evidence and discarding what is useless.

Thus the higher training of a warrior is to choose his or her goals wisely. Should warriors waste their whole life in pursuit of a goal that may be unattainable? Perhaps. Sometimes the fight, even without a final victory, is a triumph in itself, a statement of the human desire for justice or freedom. Or, even if victory is likely, the warrior must calculate whether it will be worth what may be destroyed along the way. A warrior knows when to avoid a fight and also when the real wisdom is to walk away from a battle without regret.

INTERPRETATIONS

Life tasks: *You are fighting for what you want, but remember that a fight need not be a terrible struggle. The more accurately you act, the less wear and tear to yourself. Be ready to chop out dead wood and to keep only what is genuinely useful. This is no time for misplaced sentiment.*

Possible meanings: *A battle or conflict. Trouble which must be faced. An opponent. Discrimination. Rigorous training. The need to act decisively.*

THE CARDS

The Victor

ובד מק פס

Wheel 7
Suit: FIRE
COMPANION CARDS:
*The Heart, The Warrior,
The Treasury*

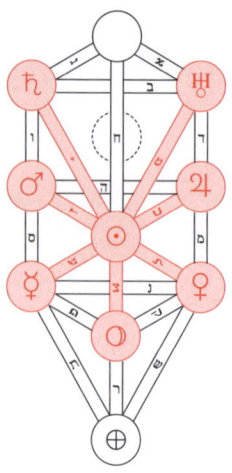

ORACLE

When people fall prey to empty and idle talk, they also fall into isolation. They forget that they are human beings, and they turn their heads away from that which they truly know. They look forever upon the echoes and images of illusion. But he who can put an end to all lies, to all concoctions and fabrications – he is the victor.

COMMENTARY

The victor may allow him or herself a few moments of triumph, but this should never be prolonged. The real knowledge of victory is in one's own heart. If you act and conquer in accordance with your own conscience, it will remain with you not as glee, but as a sense of peace. You have done what was necessary, no more and no less. When a person continually asks others to recognize his or her victory, the conquest has no true value. Triumphal arches are an empty form of architecture, serving no practical function except to swell the pompous illusions of a country and its leaders. All they do is to form a foolish frame for the conqueror and his entourage.

In everyday life, we may assume that battles and victories are far from our normal experience. Not so: who managed to get the last seat on the bus? Which cat secured the titbit? Skirmishes and conquests are taking place all the time. Even a sweet old lady can use the appeal of her fragility to secure preferential treatment. Everyone uses whatever means they have to to win, and the best victor is one who can lose and laugh when necessary. A good victor also acknowledges the role of luck and will respect those who fought against him.

All sorts of things help to teach people the knowledge of winning and losing; they are embedded in our culture and include games of chance, sports matches or public debates. They help us to adapt to a world of flux where sometimes we can win through and sometimes we can just hold onto what we know to be true.

INTERPRETATIONS

Life tasks: *You may be enjoying a moment of triumph, but there is a new challenge around the corner, so be ready to face it when it comes. No permanent stability is ever created by winning; the wheel turns again and the winners and losers change places. You must decide whether to fight to keep what you have or give in to the change and look for fresh potential within that.*

Possible meanings: *Success, triumph, conquest. Responsibilities that you must take on because of your success. Someone who has usurped you. A person who can act on your behalf. A champion. Settlement of a dispute.*

The Treasury

מד בו ספק

Wheel 7
Suit: AIR

COMPANION CARDS:
The Heart, The Warrior, The Victor

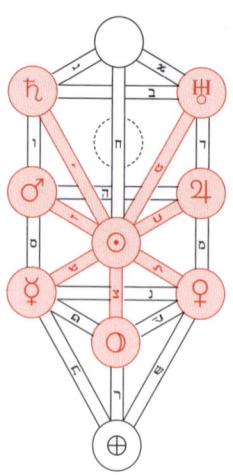

ORACLE
Into the treasury are brought the taxes, and the people are taxed according to their wealth. And when all dues have been received and the treasury is full, then its coffers are opened for all men to use. The sun is the wealth of the universe, the heart is the wealth of a human being, but nobody can receive unless he or she has already given.

COMMENTARY
Wealth must circulate through society like blood through the veins. Governments impose taxes to raise funds for the good of all. At least, that is the theory. But society will always be the final arbitrator of whether a tax is fair or not. Governments can fall for imposing what people perceive to be a totally unjust tax. Societies are happy for their monarchs to be wealthy, as long as they feel that this wealth is held in trust for the nation and will be given back to the people in time of need. The treasury is not restricted to nations either: tribal societies sometimes have a treasury where a share of the harvest is collected, to be distributed when individual supplies run low. While the chief holds the granary, the monarch her palaces and gold, and the governments our taxes, we can

feel a sense of pride in the wealth of our society. Wealth held in trust creates majesty, just as the gold ornament in churches evokes the riches of paradise.

If we understand the message of the treasury, we will know that it may be better to conserve resources and build up a store of wealth. It isn't always appropriate to give out money on demand. The same goes for our energy and talents: they shouldn't be used randomly here and there. In order to create something really splendid, we may need to hold back until the time is right and then give fully of ourselves.

Everyone loves to think about the treasury – what might be there and what splendours lie within its coffers. It seems to contain more than was put into it. It creates a sense of abundance and brings wellbeing to a community.

INTERPRETATIONS

Life tasks: *You are in a position where you have a wealth of resources at your disposal. You are gathering more into your treasury, and you need to decide how long to hold that current wealth for, and when to spend and disperse it again. But instead of just counting up your riches, ponder on the dazzling display that they make, and on the inner meaning of such wealth.*

Possible meanings: *A cornucopia of riches. The resources that you need are available. Good fortune. Plenty of money. A position looking after the resources or wealth of others. Working with exotic, rich materials. Finding hidden treasures.*

The Marker

הסמנ

Wheel 8
Suit: EARTH
COMPANION CARDS:
The Thaw, The Test, The Sign

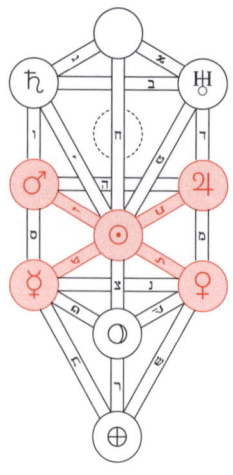

ORACLE

What marks out one thing from another? When it cannot be divided into anything else, without becoming something else, then you have found the marker of its identity. Its essence is manifest to you. Here lies integrity. Understand this, and all else can be released to the edges of the wheel and beyond, to be dissolved or absorbed in the processing of experience.

COMMENTARY

If we could not distinguish one thing from another, we could not live. We have to know that this is a chair, not a cup; we cannot perceive the object as a whirl of atoms. When the cup is smashed, it is no longer a cup. Maybe if the damage is slight, it is a 'broken cup', but beyond that only the archaeologist can resurrect the form as a ghost of the past.

We are purveyors of identity. This bird ... that stamp ... this sea shell ... that train ... all are markers of the collector's enthusiasm. Children learn with delight to name and distinguish: 'lion ... shoe ... Daddy'. Some say that this is because it gives them power over the world, but maybe that comes later. To name is to know, and to know is to love. To know can also be to fear, because our own identity fears any other identity which threatens it. But being able to name your enemy diminishes its power, or at least limits it within recognized boundaries.

When you are faced with a threat to your identity, you may ask yourself: What am I? If this attack only comes as a criticism of your personality, you may suffer hurt feelings, but your self-love will work fast to repair the damage. If it is at the level of Tiferet, where your real identity resides, the blow to confidence is more severe. It may be a criticism of the fundamental role you play in life, and the shock causes you to question who you really are. The person you are in essence is bound up with your creative output in life – or is it? There are people who have suffered terrible loss, injury, or ruin of reputation, but who have yet come through with renewed strength. Ultimately, none of these things can take away the essence of being.

INTERPRETATIONS

Life tasks: *It is time to know yourself better. Strip away all false expectations, both yours and those of others. Discover the resonance and meaning of your name when it is spoken out loud. Do not be afraid to find yourself.*

Possible meanings: *Illusion that must be banished. A badge, token, identifying mark. A gift with an inner meaning. A clue. Recognition. Choosing a name. Identifying a person. Something which defines you or marks your limits.*

The Thaw

הנמס

Wheel 8
Suit: WATER
COMPANION CARDS:
*The Marker, The Test,
The Sign*

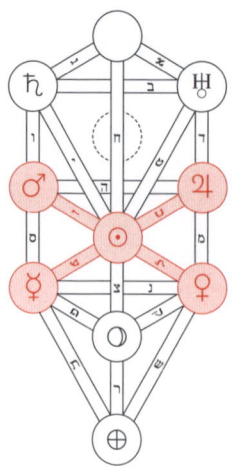

ORACLE

From flowing action comes growth. It rises and builds great structures, but at its zenith it pauses, as the impetus that propelled it is now spent. Now it must find something upon which to rest its inert weight. But however strong the support, it will inevitably give way. Then the structure will crack and its energies spill out and ebb away.

COMMENTARY

Here there is a subtle interplay between the forces of growth and the forms that this growth takes. As growth reaches its peak, the energy crystallizes into form. The form lingers, but without further input of energy, it will eventually give way and release any remaining energy contained there. Great civilizations have created extraordinary buildings – palaces and castles, pyramids and temples. But when the civilizations die, so very often their buildings are left to crumble away too, unless later generations decide to rescue them. Sculpted snowdrifts melt into water, and the force of the melting snow swells rivers and sweeps away bridges. Thaws may be slow or sudden, destructive or energizing, but they are all processes of release.

At the time of dissolution, you will find that new possibilities open to you. A marriage decays, a job collapses or a creative project crumbles away into the dust – all these may cause a great shake-up in your life, but they will also release energy. Do not stay loyal to the pain of that collapse, let that pass after you have paid due respect to what was. There is no such thing as emptiness. Even when you fear that the pain of loss will be replaced by a dull meaninglessness, new forces are gathering to create all over again. You cannot use them to replace the old, so listen and watch, and take note of what they will bring you.

Certain thaws just happen, as is in the nature of things, but we can be instrumental in setting off other forms of release. Sometimes we need to break down old structures to provide a new impetus to go forward. Some people are addicted to this, and no sooner have they built something up, than they knock it down in order to find that excitement all over again. This is an abuse of energy, and leads to diminishing returns.

INTERPRETATIONS

Life tasks: *This may be a time to wait while the process of change takes its course. Whatever has been set in motion cannot now be halted. Don't waste energy trying to stop or accelerate it, that would only make matters more complicated, just try to steer your boat calmly on the current.*

Possible meanings: *Release. Removing a blockage. A new flow of ideas. Renewed creative energy. Indiscreet speech, the telling of secrets. The dissolution of a relationship.*

The Test

מנסה

Wheel 8
Suit: FIRE
COMPANION CARDS:
The Marker, The Thaw, The Sign

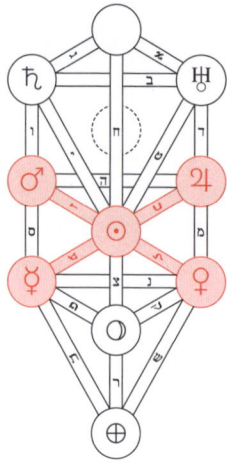

ORACLE

The test is always to be what you are. The present moment always demands that you should be what you have become. No matter what the excuse, what the rationale, this is what faces you. Words are fine long clothes that hide you from the sight of your fellows, but they also trip you up as you grasp at life.

COMMENTARY

This card is about truth. The naked truth of your being may not be something that you wish to reveal very often. It is powerful, yet vulnerable. It is rare to see someone just as they are. Social interaction demands niceties, evasions, mild lies and flattery. We protect others from the full force of our being, and also protect ourselves from possible scorn or attack. The danger is that we may conceal the truth even from ourselves. Then, when we rush forward eagerly to embrace something, we are tripped up by the image we've created of ourselves. Someone thinks of you as wise – so you don't show that you are confused. Someone believes you are peaceable – so you hide your anger. If you put too much energy into promoting a false image, it will suck up the sun and leave you with little light to spare.

THE TEST

The test of being who you are in the moment is a hard one. Even the person who tries to be honest, may still imagine him or herself to be younger, cleverer, taller or better-looking than in reality. When you catch sight of your image unexpectedly in a mirror, who is it that reacts? At that moment, you are distanced from your image and you dwell in your own essence. Your shock comes from the knowledge that you are not that image, and yet you are responsible for it. Your real centre of being is something else, not the picture in the mirror, but nevertheless your history is written on your face – and there may be rather more of it there than you would like!

If you are insulted, move past the insult, beyond the defiance and the hurt to see what is truly behind it. Your essence cannot really be insulted, because it has no self-regard. It is what it is.

INTERPRETATIONS

Life tasks: *You may be tested in some very searching ways. Keep your own centre of balance, be truthful to yourself and you will survive. You do not have to tell everybody else all your real thoughts and feelings. The real test is an inner one, and if you act with integrity, matters around you will clear up.*

Possible meanings: *An exam or test. An inspector or inspection. Proving your worth. The need to adapt to changed circumstances without compromising your integrity. A plan or project will be tested for its validity.*

THE CARDS

The Sign

מהנס

Wheel 8
Suit: AIR
COMPANION CARDS:
*The Marker, The Thaw,
The Test*

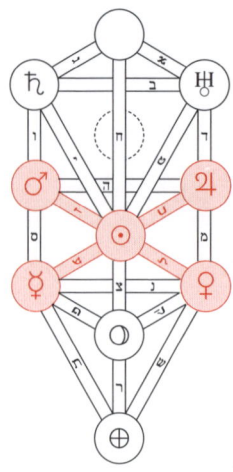

ORACLE

Every action, feeling and presentiment has a sign. A sign to tell those who cannot see. A sign to retell the story to those who listen and breathe in its wonder. A sign to forewarn those who know and wait. The face of every person is a sign of their soul. But signs tell only of what they know to be, they do not make or create knowledge.

COMMENTARY

Signs and omens are what they are: in one sense, you cannot really interpret them, in another, their interpretations are dependent upon the people who witness them. Three people, for example, see the same brilliant, intense winter sunset, the sun low and huge on the horizon, like a red ball of glowing fire. But each sees it as a sign of something different. A child in the street is frightened by its intensity, has seen nothing like it before and thinks it is a sign that the world is about to end. A farmer sees this sunset and is delighted, believing that it is a sign of good weather for tomorrow. An artist sees the same sunset and takes it as a sign leading her to the next painting, spying in it the transcendent beauty that should be captured on canvas. All three visions of the sunset are real, but all are dependent upon the knowledge and expectations of the individual.

Such a sunset is a relatively common occurrence, but there are out-of-the-ordinary signs too. There are strange appearances of birds and animals, celestial phenomena, reports of angels and ghosts, of extraordinary dreams, apparitions and visions. It may be one person who witnesses them or many, but their interpretation will still depend upon the view of each beholder. In times gone by, kings appointed astrologers, oracles, seers and diviners to interpret the signs collectively for the nation. Those people today who cherish such epiphanies and who train their attention to catch them, will see more signs than others. But seeing is one thing and interpretation another. Interpretations are always angled and may reduce the way in which you experience the intrinsic power of the sign.

The world we live in is a magical place, and it speaks to us through signs and symbols. Through them, we learn to put trust in the potency and life of the universe, to know that there are different levels of existence and that the higher shines through the lower.

INTERPRETATIONS

Life tasks: *Look for a sign. You cannot make the decision without reference to external powers or people. However, when you have the indications that you need, it will still be you who takes the decision.*

Possible meanings: *An unexpected event or appearance. An omen to take note of. A significant occurrence. Symbols, divination. A key word or phrase. A declaration.*

THE CARDS

The Disciple

בן מוסד

Wheel 9
Suit: EARTH
COMPANION CARDS:
The Passover, The Flag, The Court

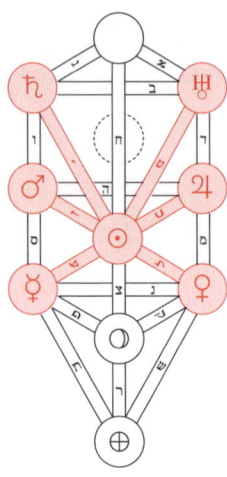

ORACLE

Sons and daughters turn a mother and a father into parents; the children of children establish a dynasty; it is the disciples who found the faith. The disciple must have even greater discernment than the teacher. The disciple's contribution is to fix the teacher's creation, as cement or clay sets hard like stone for future use.

COMMENTARY

Few people begin with an ardent desire to teach. The artist prefers to create and the business person to transact, and the mystic can't take time off contemplation to instruct others. But sometimes this need to teach presses upon us. Just as no one knows how to be a parent until he or she has children, so no one ever thinks that they really know enough to teach. The situation draws it out of us. Children, pupils and disciples all draw knowledge, understanding and wisdom out of us. They also test our patience and provoke strong judgements as well as inspiring love and compassion.

Teaching involves endless repetition. And as if that wasn't enough, the person who gives the teaching, who bestows the golden nectar of knowledge, finds that the pupils understand it differently and do other things with it. We can only give people the tools and encourage them to develop the skills. They then find their own way, grateful for how they have been equipped, but burning with their own enthusiasms and impelled by their own quests. A rigid system of teaching and knowledge will last only a generation or two at best. One that encourages future development may persist for hundreds, if not thousands, of years.

Kabbalah means 'to receive'. Ultimately, the teacher is only a channel for the teaching, and the best he or she can do is to show students how to open themselves to knowledge.

This card is of earth because all knowledge and teaching must be embodied sooner or later. The touchstone of past achievement is in the art, the architecture, the government, the science and the laws of a society. All wisdom and understanding eventually makes itself manifest, and humans are a way in which the creation can reveal itself in the visible world.

INTERPRETATIONS

Life tasks: *It is time to begin a new phase of learning. This could be formal study, but it doesn't have to be a set course. Maybe you can teach as well? There is always value in passing on what you know. If you have not studied for a while, remember that it is a discipline in itself. In a new subject, you have to be prepared to start at the bottom. But this is also wonderfully liberating.*

Possible meanings: *A teacher, a student, a training system. A course of study. Someone is eager to learn from you. Humbleness in the face of greater knowledge.*

The Passover

נסו בדמ

Wheel 9
Suit: WATER
COMPANION CARDS:
The Disciple, The Flag, The Court

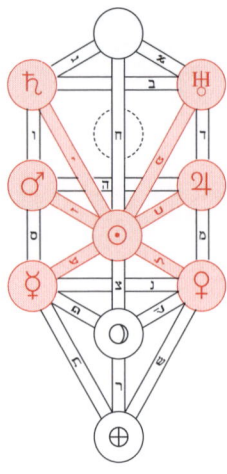

ORACLE
A sign marked in the blood of a lamb protected the Israelites when God smote down all the first-born in Egypt. Allowed by God to remain as slaves, the Israelites were exempted from his awful wrath by their faith, because they knew him as the one and true God. And this is what separated them from other men.

COMMENTARY
The Passover marks the time when the Jewish people were freed from slavery in Egypt. God told Moses and Aaron to slaughter a sheep and mark their doors with its blood; at night, the destroying power of the Lord would pass through and kill the first-born in any unmarked house. After that terrible night, not a house in Egypt was without its dead, and the Egyptians released their captives. Along with liberation came the holy command to keep the 'Lord's Passover'. God said 'You shall keep this day as a day of remembrance, and make it a pilgrim-feast, a festival of the Lord; you shall keep it generation after generation as a rule for all time.' (Exodus 12).

Each faith has its testament and the record of key events which mark it out from other beliefs. Each believes in its own image of the deity and celebrates that difference which gives the religion its identity. Although each religion may proclaim itself to be the true way, this conviction is strengthened by the recognition that there are other beliefs. If there was only one visible colour, we might not recognize it as a colour at all.

Each belief, religious or otherwise, has truth at its core, even if it is not the only and complete truth. A person must hold onto that sense of truth, even if it is opposed or mocked by others. Each religion claims to hold the key to salvation – and it does.

As a young child you may have had an experience – a dream or a revelation or a vision of an angel perhaps – which gave you a real belief in the divine. In later years, perhaps this seemed naïve. But it is worth keeping faith with that early experience, because even though you understand it differently in later years, it is still sacred. If you deny it, you cut yourself off from the roots of your being.

INTERPRETATIONS

Life tasks: *A spiritual issue is arising for you. It could concern the belief you were brought up in or your cultural background. You may need to find a way to keep faith with the essence of that, while also embracing a new understanding and a wider perspective on the world.*

Possible meanings: *The need to be careful. Danger from your enemies. Keep your own counsel, unless you are sure of the person you are speaking to. Gratitude, giving thanks for safe passage. Protecting yourself and others.*

THE CARDS

The Flag

מנס ובד

Wheel 9
Suit: FIRE

COMPANION CARDS:
*The Disciple,
The Passover, The Court*

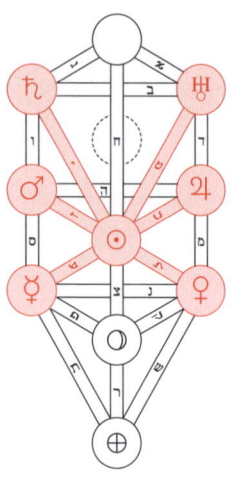

ORACLE

Everyone salutes a flag, whether they know it or not. Each of you wears on your lapel an invisible insignia, to which you owe silent allegiance. But people become over-excited by the profusion of flags, especially when there are many of the same kind flying at once. They love to see the waving and the marching, and to shout and cheer. Then they see only the flag and forget what it is for.

COMMENTARY

Causes are contentious. What starts off as a rousing gathering can turn into an ugly riot. In theory, a flag harnesses all the collective energy and unifies people under a common purpose or identity. However, a lot can go wrong; there may be opposing flags out on the streets or people marching under the same flag may start squabbling about what they are really there for. A flag is created as a symbol of the common cause, giving it extra power and focus. It is also a symbol of higher authority, confirming an allegiance greater than that of people who simply share an opinion. In suitable arenas, flag-bearers take delight in challenging others who carry a different flag. In the best cases, this gives us tournaments and matches, pageantry, exciting contests and celebration. The sight of different flags flying together creates a colourful and energizing occasion. At worst, flags are used to bully and to provoke confrontation, as when rival political groups clash on the street. A flag can even become a physical weapon. Sometimes the flag is a sad symbol of what was, the reminder of past days of glory held by a band of dwindling adherents.

What do you feel when you see a flag flying? Does it lift your spirits, provoke you to anger or simply generate a little tired, amused cynicism? What does your attitude mean? This card is about how you respond to a cause or a statement of allegiance. No one is without allegiance: it pays to know where yours lies.

It is possible to go deeper into the symbolism of the flag or badge. How has the choice of colours and image been arrived at? There is power in simplicity, and in combining contrasting features held strongly and securely together.

INTERPRETATIONS

Life tasks: *You are bound up in a cause or project which demands your allegiance. This is a good way of focusing your energies and encouraging others to join you if needs be. But it is also a limiting factor, requiring steady belief and commitment. You should consider whether it could confine you too much in the long run.*

Possible meanings: *A mark of recognition. Social or political cause. A question to do with nationality or cultural background. A badge of office. The need to focus objectives. A declaration.*

THE CARDS

The Court

דון מסב

Wheel 9
Suit: AIR
COMPANION CARDS:
*The Disciple,
The Passover, The Flag*

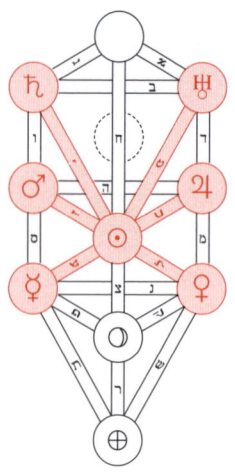

ORACLE

The supreme court of the kingdom endorses the decisions of the crown. It reflects those wishes and also burnishes its own will, so that the reflected image of the crown can shine there more brightly. The purer and brighter this image, the stronger is the court and the stronger the kingdom. The court must give judgements and advice that exalt the crown, so that it almost disappears within its own brilliance. In a well-governed kingdom, the crown must never be seen to act.

COMMENTARY

A 'Crown Court' is described in this oracle, where the court is directly answerable to the monarch and the monarch to God, and thus the court itself is a sacred instrument for dispensing justice. This principle can be said to underlie all kinds of courts, at local and national level, both in republics and in monarchies. But in this context, it also refers to the Tree of Life, where the highest sefira, Keter, is described as the Crown. In this wheel, the Crown is not present, but it is imminent, and will in fact appear in the next set of cards.

This brings us to a more personal interpretation of the card. Sometimes what you do is put on trial. Who judges it? Your boss, your peers, the world, your family? – the list of your judges is endless. Sometimes you may have the chance to avoid judgement, if you refuse to recognize 'the court' that tries you. At other times you will have no choice, because your judges have authority over you. The judgement can be about right and wrong, but it can also be about the viability of your actions, and your rights. However, even in a situation where there is no wrongdoing, there is always a moral base for judgement. Everything must be weighed in the balance.

None of us is above judgement. The views of others are very rarely entirely wrong. The court is there to help us present evidence in the most objective light and to give the person on trial a reasonable hearing. Sentence should not be passed without trial, and a trial should be conducted in a fair manner. You owe it to others to give them a fair hearing, as they do to you.

INTERPRETATIONS

Life tasks: *What you do is not entirely free of constraints. You must recognize the right of others to question your actions and you may have to justify yourself to them. But you also have the right to demand a fair examination of the facts and you can refer them to higher authority if necessary.*

Possible meanings: *Legal action. A court case. Judgement. Referral to superior authority. A decision that has to be made when the evidence is weighed. A clear, balanced approach. The need to examine the facts.*

The Benefactor

דאג וספקמ

Wheel 10
Suit: EARTH

COMPANION CARDS:
*Agitation, The Martyr,
The Presence*

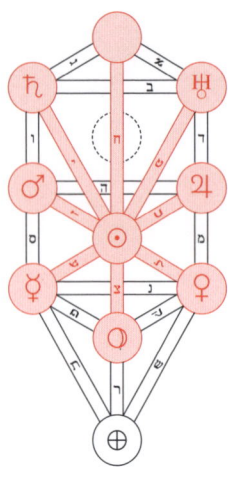

ORACLE
The person who cares and is anxious for the welfare of another, whose hand grasps their shoulder in sympathy and who claps with joy and encouragement – such a person is the benefactor. The benefactor brings an abundance of wisdom and understanding to each situation, illuminating it, meeting its insufficiencies and revealing its inherent possibilities. To be a benefactor is to receive and pass on blessings.

COMMENTARY
There are people who give you real help in life, putting fresh heart into you during difficult times. Their cheerfulness dissolves the dull, frozen fear that has taken a grip on your heart. They bring blessings from a fuller world, when your own world has diminished, and you cannot help responding to their warmth.

It is not a gift which should burden you, because it rouses your own energies rather than dominating them. The benefactor gives you a boost, which helps you to get going, without leaving an acute sense of obligation. The only obligation, perhaps, is for you to do the same for someone else when the appropriate time comes.

THE BENEFACTOR

Societies try to organize mechanisms which will provide for all of our genuine needs of health and welfare. But, as we know, institutionalized services can only go so far. Those who work for them are guided by strict codes of conduct, and they leave their tasks behind them at the end of the day. There is always a place for the benefactor, someone who will give joyously, from the core of their being.

But a benefactor must not become a tyrant of benevolence. Giving should not become a gratifying habit; it needs to keep its spontaneity. Institutionalized benefactors are called sponsors and patrons. Their services to humanity may be valuable, but they do not usually operate from the same sense of generosity. The true benefactor does not plan how to give, but responds to the needs of each situation as it arises. Benevolence should not feed the pride of the giver. Forcing someone to accept your gifts or support in order to maintain your image is wrong. If you give, give freely.

Ask yourself: who or what at this moment is your benefactor? The answers may surprise you.

INTERPRETATIONS

Life tasks: *You are in a position where you are able to give, as well as to receive. In fact, it is vital that for whatever sustenance you receive, you are able to pass on nourishment to others. This is not about counting up costs and debts, but about responding wholeheartedly to need.*

Possible meanings: *A gift. A sponsor or supporter who will help you. A person who gives you much. Something of great value that deserves recognition. A source of good luck. Your role as patron, gift-giver. A part of your life which has warmth and vitality.*

Agitation

מדאג וספק

Wheel 10
Suit: WATER

COMPANION CARDS:
The Martyr, The Presence, The Benefactor

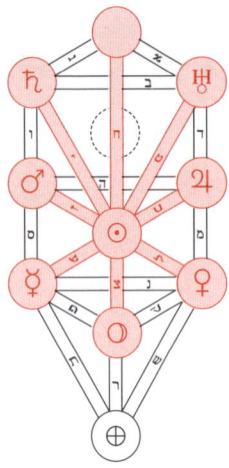

ORACLE

To be agitated is to be lost. Agitation only produces actions which perpetuate itself. To cry 'shame', to clasp a hand to your brow in remorse, to strike a clenched fist against a soft palm, is to be defeated. When the first beads of sweat appear, they must be wiped away, the brow smoothed and the breath deepened. Then, follow that which you have learnt, or go and be taught it now.

COMMENTARY

Dealing with anxiety is a problem for many people, especially those who are expected to perform to a high standard, and who have high expectations of themselves. Sometimes a traumatic incident makes it doubly difficult to face the world without trembling. It is a double-edged situation, because this agitation is almost a religious experience. It is the acknowledgement of a power beyond your own. The audience that awaits you, or the boss who will scrutinize your work, are symbols of the attentive power that maintains the universe. The performer bows, humbled by such a sense of greatness.

Keeping your cool in such demanding situations can be immensely challenging.

Devices that help to control your anxiety one day may be useless the next. But the oracle gives us the clue that we can encourage calmness, we can reduce the symptoms of agitation, and we can employ useful skills that we have learnt. It is tempting, under pressure, to throw away caution and abandon oneself to whatever strange power seems to be possessing us. But skills are learnt for a reason. We can use them very effectively to stabilize a traumatic moment. Breathing and relaxation techniques are taught for this reason, and performers and presenters learn technical skills which will support them when under pressure. Once you are before an audience, you will need all the techniques you can muster.

Agitation can also arise when you are sensitively attuned to a situation, perhaps receiving psychic impressions from it. Learn to read your own signals and symptoms. What has disturbed you? Why has your breathing quickened? Perhaps it is the atmosphere or the place, or something unusual is about to happen. We have very acute senses, if we will allow them to work for us.

INTERPRETATIONS

Life tasks: *You may be going through a period of upset and disturbance. Your sense of yourself has been shaken; you are unclear about the future. Learn to live with this agitation, just for a while. Don't suppress it or make too much out of it either. What can you see in the water? Maybe just fragments of light, for the moment. But sooner or later, an image will form there.*

Possible meanings: *A shake up. Someone who is upset or who may cause trouble for others. A cause for worry. A transition phase. Anxiety, self-doubt.*

The Martyr

קם דאג וסף

Wheel 10
Suit: FIRE
COMPANION CARDS:
*The Benefactor,
Agitation, The Presence*

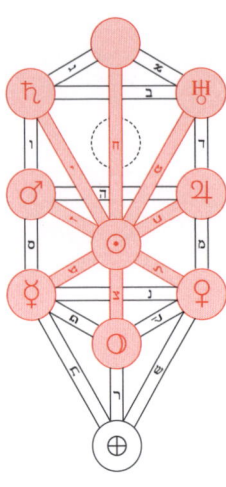

ORACLE
Within the heart, a tremble is felt, and then the calm breath gives way to a sharp intake of breath. All you desire seems about to slip out of reach. If you trip at the threshold, you are lost. For your imbalance is the force which can push you witlessly into useless annihilation.

COMMENTARY
Martyrdom is a controversial state. Some people believe it to be the ultimate mark of faith, while others consider it a waste of a life. The oracle suggests a rather different view: that if you are martyred, it is your own imbalance that has caused it. The game was already lost. Maybe some religious martyrs simply decided to make their fall loud and crashing, sacrificing themselves to that end as effectively as possible. If you are going to die in this way, then you want that death to create maximum impact for your cause.

But here we can safely assume that the martyr refers to a more usual state of being, not to a dramatic death. 'Don't be such a martyr' is a common reproach, and suggests someone who is deliberately creating a burden for themselves. Here, as the oracle proclaims – the game is up. It is a last strategy in a losing battle. At this point, the person had better withdraw, turn their attitude around and try to come back out of it with a cheerful face. Although beware the smiling martyrs, for they are even more dangerous to themselves and others.

If we can acknowledge our own disappointment and upset, then maybe we will not need to become martyrs. That loss of balance is when we try to pin the blame on others. Recovering balance means recovering our true knowledge of the situation, for better or worse. This card is about taking responsibility for our actions. It is about acknowledging the part we play in creating any situation that we find ourselves in. Becoming a martyr will not free you, even if it brings you the attention and sympathy you crave. But ultimately, martyrdom is simply a prison. Martyrs are enshrined, but no one remembers their personalities or their individual creativity – all that is remembered is the tragic way in which they met their end.

INTERPRETATIONS

Life tasks: *You are on a threshold and you do not yet know if you can pass over it. Perhaps you will succeed, perhaps you will lose. Be ready to accept the result, whichever way it goes. If you lose, why waste useful energy mourning your loss and forcing others to acknowledge it? It is best to move on.*

Possible meanings: *A complaint. A person who forces their problems upon you. Uncertainty. Volatile emotions, which could turn negative if not restrained. Risk. The possibility of great rewards or severe losses. A sacrifice. A lost cause.*

The Presence

סוג אד מקף

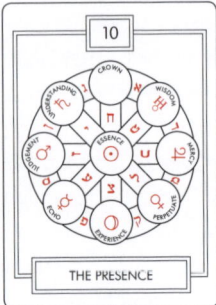

Wheel 10
Suit: AIR
COMPANION CARDS:
*The Benefactor,
Agitation, The Martyr*

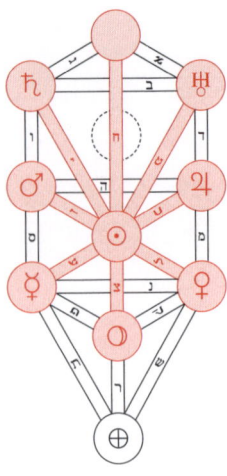

ORACLE
The first act of cultivation is to set stakes around a piece of land. Then you must remove all the weeds and dissolute plants, for they drain away the soil's energy. Then thinly sow the seeds of presence.

COMMENTARY
This is the acknowledgement of a presence greater than our own individual consciousness. But even the sense of a separate, personal consciousness is a kind of illusion. Where does it begin and end? How is it that we can sometimes feel what another person is feeling? Because in one way, we are already a part of that. But we cannot lay claim to it. The duality of 'the one and the other', I and not-I, is laid down at the core of the universe. These differences are necessary, for without them, nothing could be created. Kabbalah teaches us how these energies are differentiated, so that we can understand the components of creation. But as human beings, we also have within us the blueprint of the whole Tree of Life, and thus we can recognize the higher powers which have a place within us too. We have our own version of wisdom and understanding, even though it is limited. We also have the possibility

of developing this wisdom and understanding, and for this, the image of making a garden is very relevant. But we can only sow seeds, not force growth. We try to make the best conditions for the garden to flourish.

On the diagram of the Tree of Life, the Garden of Eden – the primordial garden of paradise – lies between Understanding, Wisdom, Judgement and Mercy. We can only gain access to it when the thoughts, fancies and chatter of Echo and Perpetuate are stilled. Then the mind calms down, and becomes receptive. We must not be afraid of working the garden, staking out the terrain, and preparing the soil. Then the Crown (Keter), the presence, can be invited to grow there.

In daily life, there are times when it is best to put down your tools, stop your efforts for a while, and simply wait and watch. Thus, you can attune yourself to the flow of conditions and to sense when a period of growth is beginning.

INTERPRETATIONS

Life tasks: *You need to create a period of calm and reflection for yourself. This could be on a daily basis or signify taking a retreat or just a time of relative inactivity. But while the outer activity is stilled, the mind should stay awake and alert. It is not a time of sleep. However busy your life, you can find time to do this. The seeds you sow like this will flourish later.*

Possible meanings: *A switch from everyday concerns to spiritual ones. A person with a strong presence or charisma. Retreat, meditation, contemplation. Choosing the right terrain in which to begin a new project.*

The Return

אדם נסוג

Wheel 11
Suit: EARTH
COMPANION CARDS:
The Cauldron,
Man of Blood, The Veil

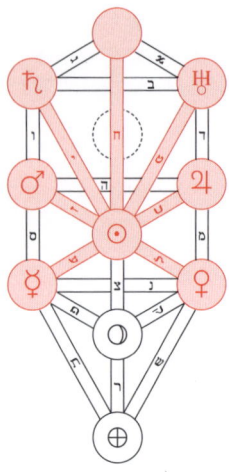

ORACLE

From seed to fruition, from fruition again to seed. Ideas must become reality, and reality, weary of its existence, turns again to ideas. You must eventually return to source, in order to validate your existence. You cannot live without roots, just as you cannot live without sun-seeking branches. To deny either will leave you withered and wilting upon the parched soil.

COMMENTARY

The Tree of Life contains the great outward and inward cycle of creation. On the outward half, we forge ahead and expand our lives and experience. On the return path, we the distil that experience, understanding where we have come from and what has been achieved in our lifetime. All cycles are similar, so that a cosmic cycle is paralleled in a human lifetime, and within a lifetime, thousands of smaller cycles also carry that blueprint. Every new project that you launch has its expansive, creative phase and its consolidating, finalizing phase. A woman's monthly cycle carries the fresh, revitalized energy of the early phase, followed by fullness and fertility at mid-cycle and then the ebbing energy that finally ends in a flow of blood. Each planet has its own cycle, mapped by astrologers who interpret their meaning. A horoscope is a moment captured and interpreted from the flows of planetary time. Jupiter cycles mark the patterns of creative endeavour, the great Saturn cycles of twenty-nine years slowly etch the learning curves of responsibility and understanding, while the moon's waxing and waning colours the fleeting impressions and emotions of our everyday life.

On the outward part of the cycle, we forget our past, because it doesn't seem relevant. On the return half, the ebb of energy, we are aware of the roots and causes of things. Very often in later life people take an interest in their family tree or in the landscape which shaped the lives of their ancestors. The contemplation of our roots is not a sign of hopeless defeat, but an enrichment. It helps us to consolidate our achievements and to understand them. That understanding we can pass on to the next generation, to make of it what they will.

INTERPRETATIONS

Life tasks: *It is time to gather the fruit from what you have sown. You may resist, because it means moving away from the heady excitement of the early stages. But there is real satisfaction in doing this. If you want to benefit from your experience, try to understand its roots and causes as well. What you gather now can be of enormous use to you in the future.*

Possible meanings: *A return to your place of origin. Closure. Something comes back to you that you thought was lost. Harvesting the fruits. Gathering together the seeds which you will sow for the next undertaking. Family history, ancestors.*

The Cauldron

אגנ מוסד

Wheel 11
Suit: WATER
COMPANION CARDS:
*The Return,
Man of Blood, The Veil*

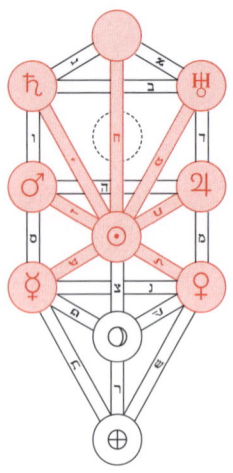

ORACLE

Within the cauldron resounds the great hollowness of antiquity. All the combinations of time and necessity have been stirred and beaten there. The course of nature has shaped its smooth, hard sides. Within it, the bubbling movements of a million processes have arisen and passed away, creating a source of fertility that never ceases.

COMMENTARY

The cauldron is one of the great symbols found in mythologies across the world. The oracle describes the sense of age, distilled wisdom and new potency that lies within it. This is a card that promises much. However, the person looking for individual glory won't find it here. All our efforts go into the cauldron and, after a few hectic moments, we cannot distinguish our contribution from another's. There is anguish in the soul when we realize that the individuality we have prized and cherished cannot last. We are a part of creation, and when our time for separate creativity is over, our energies sink into the common pool.

This is also a relevant card for working in a group. Each person who comes to a group must be willing to contribute to the general sum of knowledge. If you were a member of a tribe, think what an incredible store of wisdom and experience would be created through the generations. You would rely on it utterly for your existence. Learning how to distinguish wholesome plants from poisonous ones, how to hunt and gather, how to build shelter and how to treat illness, would all be taught to you. The myths of your people would carry knowledge of the spirit world and memories of the ancestors. Rituals condense the knowledge of the cauldron, and impart it directly to you the way that intoxicating liquor stimulates your blood. In our current day cult of individuality, we tend to forget the knowledge of our peers and that of the generations which have preceded us. We need to make our own contribution willingly, and without regret.

Time and Nature are great processors. In our own minds, experience will be distilled and our only work is to make sure that the flows are unchecked and that the bubbling and simmering can continue unimpeded. Trust to time to heal and Nature to replenish your vitality.

INTERPRETATIONS

Life tasks: *You have great resources at your disposal. Perhaps you will have to put aside your personal ambitions to use them. Why hang onto your own notions of how something must be done, when you can tap into a source of wisdom like this? This is not the time for insisting on your individual approach. Use the bounty that you have been blessed with.*

Possible meanings: *Energy. Dipping into history. Trust in the healing powers of Nature. A deep source of love. Wellbeing. Many blessings.*

Man of Blood

גא דם נסו

Wheel 11
Suit: FIRE
COMPANION CARDS:
*The Return,
The Cauldron, The Veil*

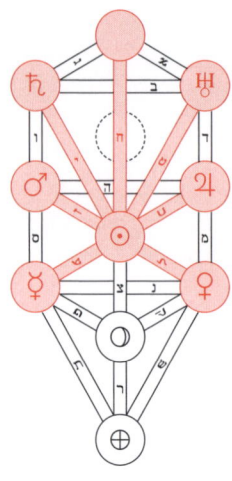

ORACLE

The life flow of a human being is in the blood. It carries oxygen and food, without which life would ebb away. Blood contains the stamp of heredity, sustains present existence and is passed on to progeny. For a man, it is the proud culmination of ancestry. A woman knows her children through the blood of her body, but a man knows his place and that of his children through his blood line.

COMMENTARY

The meaning of this card has to do with pride – pride in what you are and what has made you. In some societies, the more children you have, the higher you rank. A childless woman is looked on with pity, and the man without offspring can be an object of suspicion. Children do help to define who you are, and practically all parents are passionately proud of their children.

Here the centre of the wheel asserts its identity with pride, but defines it through lineage of being. Ancestors and children are a way of defining lineage, but so also are a line of teaching or a tradition that one partakes in. All these can be sources of pride. Pride can be egotistical, but it also brings a kind of nobility.

The oracle suggests that pride is more of a male characteristic. This may be so, but it is, of course, not exclusive to men. Perhaps it is displayed more openly by men, because they need to assert and prove their achievements to a greater extent. Women have natural knowledge of their children, from being pregnant and giving birth, and their line stretches back through all the mothers that have come before them.

Even this is not straightforward, though. There are all kinds of ways of defining heredity. The recognized line may pass through the father, the mother, or even the mother's brother, but today's births from surrogate mothers and sperm donor fathers bring new challenges in defining the blood line.

Pride would like to assume that everything is fixed, and the order of things is immutable. Pride has a tendency to become rigid, but in fact it should be supple, even if it is strong as steel.

INTERPRETATIONS

Life tasks: *Your pride in your achievements may be justified, but check that it is not also limiting you. If you talk about your success too much, people will stop listening to you. Try to be confident in your own self-worth without looking for ways to boost it all the time. But don't indulge in doubt, because other people may be relying on you.*

Possible meanings: *Family matters. Parents and children. A blood tie. Pride. Genetics, biology, bloodlines, stockbreeding. An injury to be healed. Acknowledgement of success. Award or prize.*

The Veil

מן סוג אד

Wheel 11
Suit: AIR
COMPANION CARDS:
The Return, The Cauldron, Man of Blood

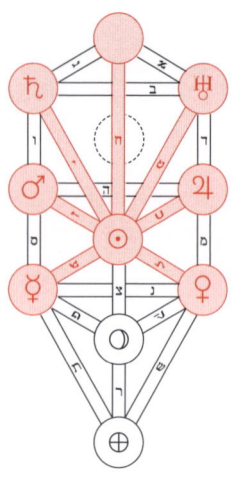

ORACLE

When the veil descended, men revered what it covered. And as time went on it seemed to hide more and more and was revered still more. Then, when it was heavy with age, young men fresh and arrogant demanded the removal of the veil and demanded to see what was hidden. For they said that whatever is hidden from the people cannot be for the common good. In the thunder and lightning of indignation, the veil was torn down. Nothing lay beyond. At first the young men were startled, but then they laughed jubilantly at the absurd fraud they thought they had uncovered. And the old men grieved, cursing the young men because they had destroyed the veil.

COMMENTARY

This oracle scarcely needs a commentary, because it paints such a vivid and recognizable picture of veneration and desecration. What one generation reveres, the next wishes to tear down. Impulsive and literally minded people do not understand the subtle nuances that others have sought to embody in sacred ritual. It is also a battle between materiality and spirituality.

Most of us have been on both sides of the struggle at one time or another. It would be wrong to suggest that young people have no sensitivity, because the real drive operating here is the discovery of the divine for oneself. The old ways can seem contrived and empty – in this story, emptiness is discovered and considered to be 'nothing'. But as most traditions tell us, 'nothing' can be the divine potency, without form but containing everything in essence. Each person and each generation tries to give form to that potency. Even the young men who tore down the veil were inspired by the search for the sacred, which they expected to find beyond the veil. The iconoclasts are paving the way for their own creations. In turn, those too will become outdated.

Yet there must be some stability in the order. If one change gives way to another too quickly, no one can do their necessary work. People must be given time to distil wisdom and understanding from their efforts, and pass it on to those who come after them.

INTERPRETATIONS

Life tasks: *There are sacred areas of your life which you are afraid to examine. But perhaps you are now strong enough to explore them. It is better to learn about them yourself, than to wait until some outside force tears them apart. These are your values, and they have real meaning for you, even if they need to be stripped of the illusions which surround them.*

Possible meanings: *Sudden overthrow of authority. A sense of mystery. A secret to be revealed. Radical new ideas and innovations. An upset between older and younger people. An issue of truth and lies.*

THE CARDS

The Gambler אוה גד

Wheel 12
Suit: EARTH
COMPANION CARDS:
*Concern, Pride,
The Society*

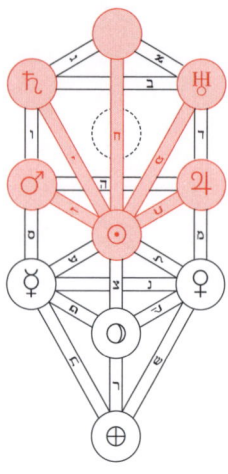

ORACLE
The gambler listens, for he can tell if it is good fortune that he hears. The gambler knows, even when he is going to lose. Sometimes he listens and then rejects what he hears, inclining his head the other way.

COMMENTARY
If you are a gambler, you are not content to wait and see what life will bring. You are prepared to take risks. But you also want to be linked into the forces that determine the outcome of events, to feel yourself a part of something greater and to swim with the tides of its fortunes. Some gambling is based entirely on 'chance' – although the gambler never believes in random chance. Some gambling has elements of skill to it, which you can use in forecasting a win, such as studying the form of racehorses. And then there is intuitive risk-taking or gambling, where you cock your ear for distant rumblings, sense a mood or try to 'read' the kind of energy that is present.

One thing we can learn from gambling is that it is very hard to produce an entirely random result. Organizers of lotteries go to tremendous lengths to ensure that the numbers picked cannot be influenced by any known bias or action. Even so, as the oracle says, some gamblers simply know when their number is going to come up. Harder still is to pick the right number in advance, but there are those who claim to have had that insight. Once you start taking such risks, and winning, gambling can be hard to stop. The odds are set against you in formalized gambling, but who is to say that the gambles you take in life will not pay off?

The accomplished gambler is one who knows how to listen to intuition, which will communicate that knowledge which is just beyond our normal comprehension. Such a gambler does not always expect to win, and indeed will sometimes have to lose just to keep that gateway to intuition open. But there is a price to pay: you will never be an innocent in matters of luck again. The wise gambler knows when it is time to retreat from the game.

INTERPRETATIONS

Life tasks: *You may need to take a gamble in order to make further progress. You can trust your intuition to give you some guidance as to how and when, because you do have some sense of what is going on. But there are no guarantees. If you are waiting for certainty, you will have to wait forever. Be ready to act, but choose your moment wisely.*

Possible meanings: *A risk – a gamble. Luck. Someone who is taking risks secretly. The opportunity to take a chance and get out of a rut. Speculation with money. The need to trust your intuition.*

Concern

הדואג

Wheel 12
Suit: WATER
COMPANION CARDS:
*The Gambler, Pride,
The Society*

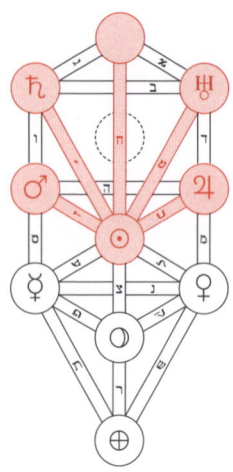

ORACLE

Be ready to recognize whatever is strong and dependable, even if it does not have the form of ordinary reality. Be prepared to multiply its manifestations, so that it can grow fully to its limits. But recognize its quality without pride or covetousness. This is the highest degree of concern.

COMMENTARY

This oracle shows that concern is not the same as anxiety, and that it is about having insight into the real nature of a situation. It can mean understanding future potential, even when there is very little evidence to go on at the present time. Concern actively, but unselfishly, tries to foster that potential. For example, if we become involved in another person's situation, then we have to try and stand back, and not take anything from it for ourselves.

In practical terms though, concern is often allied to worry. Worry is the mechanism by which we are alerted to a problem that needs our attention. Worry in itself does not have any value, but it acts to help us keep the problem in mind and to chew over possible solutions until something is resolved.

Divination is a way of structuring our concern, and of giving us a clearer perspective on a situation. A layout of the cards exposes inherent patterns, like symbols on a woven carpet, so that out of apparent chaos, order emerges. Many of the cards help us go much deeper than our usual preoccupations, and give us a chance to see not just the surface of events, but also their underlying causes. When we can see that there is meaning in what seemed to be a random assault of events, it brings relief. Understanding eases worry, and wisdom begins to reveal possibilities to us.

If this card comes up in a reading, it may well indicate an area of anxiety, but it indicates the need to dig deeper, to find out why. It demands that we look at the situation afresh and see its possibilities, not only its shortcomings. Concern gives you faith that you have the ability to work with the process of events, not merely be swept along by them.

INTERPRETATIONS

Life tasks: *If you are worried, find out why. Do this by deepening your understanding, not by ceaseless analysis. Try to see the bigger picture and what is happening on a larger scale. Consult a wise advisor if you like, but remember that you will have to take any action yourself. Discover what you cannot change and then you will have the freedom to decide what you can do to help the situation.*

Possible meanings: *A problem. An issue that should be looked at. Worry. Helping others. Something which has been neglected and is now causing trouble. The possibility of expanding a limited situation into one with more scope.*

Pride

גא הוד

Wheel 12
Suit: FIRE

COMPANION CARDS:
*The Gambler, Concern,
The Society*

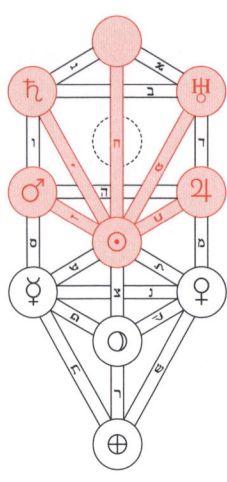

ORACLE

Out of knowledge and adoration come splendour and majesty. Like the sun, this splendour casts its radiance far, reaching even towards its own source. But if Pride seeks to eclipse its creator, then, like a sun, its great heat will grow more intense, its pride more vigorous, until its hunger forces it to turn and consume itself. Then, like a burnt-out star, it shrinks and fades away, becoming a wizened dwarf.

COMMENTARY

Everything has a life span, even our own sun. Anything that is dazzling now will one day burn out. The person who forgets that powers are lent, not possessed, will be in for a shock when they begin to decline. The oracle warns us not to take too much pride in our own achievements. What starts out as gratitude and exuberance following a triumph, can end up as unbearable conceit.

The pride portrayed on this card does arise out of true attainment, however. Where the sun, Tiferet, stands at the centre, there is genuine knowledge. Adorn - the second meaning of Tiferet - conveys the beauty and glory that can be present when we are exultant. To find the way to Tiferet, to the inner light and essence of our being, is a real achievement in itself. The world of Sense and Experience tends to keep us bobbing in the world of imagination and personality, limited by sensory experience and the emotions that continually arise out of our interactions. At Tiferet you know who you are, but analysis of that knowledge is not necessary. Confidence comes your way.

But there are three levels of Tiferet – the child, the strong youth and finally a regal king or queen. And, unlike the natural process of growing up, the pathway to maturing spiritually demands constant effort and input. It will not happen of its own accord. For this, it is necessary to take responsibility for one's actions. Pride in our achievements can limit our progress and may seem pitifully amusing to those of greater experience, just as adults chuckle at a child's first words, when it thinks that it has mastered speech.

INTERPRETATIONS

Life tasks: *You may be in for a shock, unless you can step back and look at your position with a more objective eye. You cannot rely on past achievements to keep you going, and if you try to hold onto the power that they gave you, it may be taken away from you altogether. Better to hand over to others, at least in some degree, and keep only what you really need for yourself.*

Possible meanings: *Conceit. The need for real assessment, not congratulation. A golden triumph which you can enjoy for a while, but not forever. Possessiveness. The public eye. A person who is blocking progress through pride.*

THE CARDS

The Society

אוגדה

Wheel 12
Suit: AIR
COMPANION CARDS:
*The Gambler, Concern,
Pride*

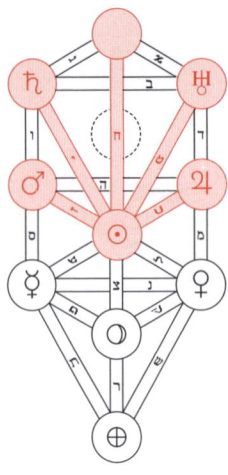

ORACLE

The society serves the human beings who are its members. The society connects them all, and is the overriding, organizing law for living which all gregarious people must observe. The society cannot accept outsiders, for these are its enemies. But without society, who can exist? Even its outcasts live by huddling in loneliness around its fringes.

COMMENTARY

There are very few true outsiders in life. We are all dependent on one another, both physically and emotionally. In some tribal societies, the ultimate punishment was to be cast out of the tribe, where you would almost certainly die, unless another tribe took you in. If society is operating smoothly, we may have the illusion that we are independent, because it doesn't impinge too noticeably on our daily lives. It doesn't interfere with our plans or stop us doing what we want to. Some cultures veer towards promoting the society as the dominant power, while others give preference to the individual. There will never be one precise way of balancing the needs of both.

This card reminds us of the network of life we participate in. It also speaks of our connections to past and future generations, to the society of humankind as a whole. In Kabbalah, there is the idea of a Great Man, known as Adam Kadmon, who represents all the people who have ever lived and who will ever live. Kabbalah teaches that we can play an active and conscious part in the body of Adam, if we so choose.

Most people, once they have satisfied their most pressing desires and ambitions, do want to make a contribution to humanity. To give from your own individuality, from your own creativity for the welfare of all, is real fulfilment. There is ultimate goodness in each person, and its natural impetus is to serve others.

We need to recognize that there can be many ways of contributing and that some of them are not physical. Prayer and contemplation is one, for though it is apparently a solitary activity, its aim is to connect to the source of life and to make a channel for the divine powers to bless the world. At the other end of the scale, a small and humble task may make a real difference, if it is carried out with kindness.

INTERPRETATIONS

Life tasks: *If you wish to be free, you must first acknowledge all the ties that bind you. Recognize the network that supports you in your individual freedom. You have received a lot of sustenance from it – is there anything you can put back into it, to create nourishment for others?*

Possible meanings: *An organization or contact network. Work for the community. Your place in the social scheme of things. Collective help from others. Your service to society.*

The Tempter

דבהו

Wheel 13
Suit: EARTH
COMPANION CARDS:
The Sorrow,
The Audience, The Myth

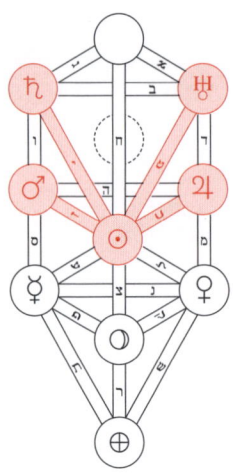

ORACLE

When you induce someone to believe, you are acting as a tempter. If you offer that person a way to wisdom and understanding and to a power beyond their comprehension, that is temptation. For in our minds, we create pictures of ourselves wielding power. But power has its own image and form, and exerts its own demands. It cannot be summoned with a snap of the fingers. Thus to tempt a person is to pander to their illusions.

COMMENTARY

Temptation can lead us into a maze of illusions. All the tempter has to do is to persuade us of the benefits of following a certain path and the desire is kindled to enter the labyrinth. It may seem a straight enough track at the beginning, but there will be many twists and turns that we did not anticipate. The tempter is usually smart enough to jump out of the way once the person has yielded to temptation.

But some temptations are helpful. The mother who tempts a sick child to eat or the employer tempting someone out of a rut into more challenging work – both are using temptation for a good purpose. If a temptation is to wake up, to partake of life, to use neglected talents, it cannot be bad – or can it? The oracle strikes a warning note, suggesting that if we believe in gaining impossible powers as a result of following the temptation, then we may be worse off. But if the temptation is a stepping-stone to higher good or knowledge, then it may be a justifiable device. We can also tempt ourselves to do things that we ought to do. We can be tempter, temptee and higher judge all in one.

The way of the Kabbalist is that of the cunning man or woman. The Kabbalist recognizes his or her own laziness and reluctance and converts these into willingness, through cunning. Temptation is a tool which we can use to persuade ourselves to do the work of clearing the weeds, on the promise of uncovering a beautiful flower beneath.

INTERPRETATIONS

Life tasks: *Are you the tempter or are you being tempted? If you are primarily the tempter – are you willing to take responsibility when those tempted follow the course you are suggesting? You will have to do that, unless you are very sure that they will take full responsibility themselves. If you are the one being tempted, look beyond the immediate benefits to the long-term implications, when the lustre has worn off the prize that you hope to win.*

Possible meanings: *A person of influence and persuasion. A moral decision to be made. The promise of something special – but it needs to be examined carefully. Someone unscrupulous. A prize, a gift, a goal that could be yours.*

The Sorrow

Wheel 13
Suit: WATER

COMPANION CARDS:
The Tempter,
The Audience, The Myth

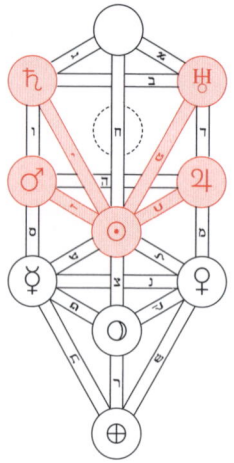

ORACLE

Within the solitude of loss lies the deepest sorrow. When the dependable collapses and the staves of security are uprooted, then the only way forward is through intuition, for you must strike home the invisible nail. But sorrow comes with that too, because it is then that you realize you are no longer as others and you can no longer claim their loyalty; you may only serve them.

COMMENTARY

Grief and loss take us deep into the furthermost reaches of our being. In Kabbalistic terms this can signify ascending to the higher reaches of the Tree of Life. The normal emotions, which reside at the level of Experience, Echo and Perpetuate, are not enough to carry the power and weight of profound loss. At such times, the loss leads us through the left-hand pillar to the terrible finality of Judgement. We want to overturn it, to undo what has been done, but we cannot. The tenderness of Mercy touches our sorrow to the quick, and so we arrive at the house of Understanding (Binah), which we may experience as an utter aloneness in the universe. Wisdom lies beyond, the renewer of life and our only hope. But it is hard to contemplate, because it produces possibilities that can wash away our careful constructions, as the tide washes away castles in the sand.

If we submit, with good grace, to Wisdom, then all may be changed. The fixed points of reference have dissolved, and we must find that invisible, intuitive point of reference to which the oracle refers. Whoever would have thought that freedom comes at such a price? And the way of recovery from sorrow is to follow the flow from that watershed, working with the knowledge that nothing is fixed, nothing is permanent, and that nothing can directly replace that loss.

If you have visited the halls of Judgement, the 'Upper Court', just once in your life, it is enough. The oracle is right: you will be different from other people and you will not be able to explain to them what you have passed through. But they will recognize the change and they will be warmed by the new compassion in you and listen respectfully to your judgements.

INTERPRETATIONS

Life tasks: *Whatever loss you are experiencing, you can or will come to terms with it. However hard the path, there is comfort which perhaps now you cannot imagine. You will lose your old way of looking at things, but when you have adjusted to that change you may find even more meaning and value in life.*

Possible meanings: *Sadness. Loss. A deep disappointment. The chance to mourn the old and to start anew. An expectation that will not be fulfilled. Working with others from compassion.*

THE CARDS

The Audience

Wheel 13
Suit: FIRE

COMPANION CARDS:
*The Tempter,
The Sorrow, The Myth*

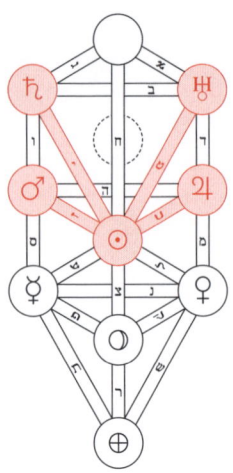

ORACLE

The house echoed with reports and responses. It shook with laughter and creaked with the toil of its inmates. They listened, inclining their heads as if to a soft-spoken rumour, and even the house itself paused. Then, out of the silence came a long and distant murmur which drew them all to itself. It was then that they became like the house, echoing with reports and responses.

COMMENTARY

What is the house that the oracle refers to? Could it be a family home, lived in for generations? Could it be a theatre, where actors and audience create noise and applause? Could it perhaps be the human skull, full of its own noise? It is a container that is capable of amplifying and resonating. In a house, the timbers can become permeated with the sounds and activities of its occupants. In a theatre, the building itself acquires a kind of mystique, so that it is praised as a perfect abode for the art that it houses. And what about the halls of meditation? As we turn our attention inwards, we become aware of the noise and chatter, murmurs and whisperings, which both tempt and plague us. But when we finally descend into silence, it is not silence after all. It has its own sound, in which we can be enfolded. Then meditation and meditator are as one.

Everyone has to be a part of the interaction in the world. Complete silence and solitude are an illusion. The way of Kabbalah is not to seal oneself off, but to open oneself up. For a while, we may believe that our new knowledge sets us apart from others. But eventually it brings us back into the field of life, with all its humming, buzzing activity. The difference is that we can now hear the music in that. If you recognize that some events arise from random causes, then you will be able to act more spontaneously yourself. If you allow the sounds of life to resonate within you, then your own voice will be more resonant. And if you accept the actions of others, you will be less enraged by them. Laughter connects us to our fellow human beings; even the saintliest men and women enjoy a good laugh.

INTERPRETATIONS

Life tasks: *Whatever you are working on needs an audience. Even your ideas need an airing, and you should ask a number of people to listen to them, so that you can gauge the overall response. You do not have to act on everyone's advice, but if you listen carefully, you may gather some valuable information, perhaps as much from what is not spoken as from the words you hear.*

Possible meanings: *The performing arts. A presentation. Seeking an audience for your ideas or activities. Being a good listener.*

THE CARDS

The Myth

Wheel 13
Suit: AIR
COMPANION CARDS:
The Tempter, The Sorrow, The Audience

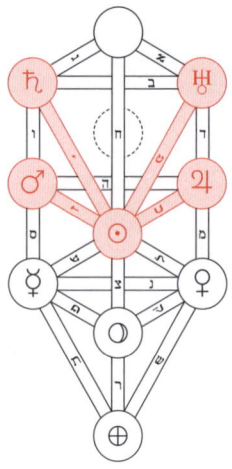

ORACLE
We call a myth something which has a past and a future, but which we have not fully experienced ourselves. And those myths may refuse to bow down to evidence and rational explanations. Perhaps then we will deny them and dismiss them as mere stories. But such tales can be remarkably tenacious and their language very compelling. How is it then that some people claim to have no interest in myths?

COMMENTARY
It is true that the word 'myth' has a double meaning. In some contexts, myth is seen as a vehicle for carrying a great truth, and in others the term myth is used to describe a collective illusion. One person's cherished myth is another's superstition. Whatever we believe in, we like to call 'truth', and whatever we consider unreal, however appealing, we label as 'myth'. Here then, we have an interplay between supreme truth and the forms that this truth clothes itself in. No one, it is said, can fully know the real powers of Wisdom, Understanding, Judgement and Mercy. But if we enter the arena they create, we can perhaps gain insight and even, on occasion, revelation. That

revelation has to be interpreted and coloured if anyone else is to have a chance of understanding it. It even needs clothing if we want to keep it in our own memory, because any knowledge you receive when you are in a higher state of consciousness is likely to slip out of your grasp when you return to everyday awareness.

Myths are the exotic and beautiful tales that are told by those who have ventured into this supernal realm. They are traveller's tales or stories that have grown from the accounts of many travellers told over the years, because the best myths do not belong to one person alone. Myths can inspire us and act as a bridge so that we in our turn may cross over into that realm.

Beware of calling your myth 'truth', and someone else's 'illusion'. The universe has many dimensions; each person is a version of the truth, and you cannot deny another person's truth. Remember, too, that a myth is a pointer – it is not literal truth – and behind it lies knowledge which has no immediate counterpart in words and images.

INTERPRETATIONS

Life tasks: *If your relationship or your work is empowered by a myth, then it will have extra energy and inspiration. But do you know what that myth is and what it is saying? You will need to test and consolidate it in the real world too.*

Possible meanings: *A question concerning religion, an ideal or a cause. A myth, story or legend. Superstitions. Means of communication. A truth which you must dress up.*

THE CARDS

The Covering ט יח

Wheel 14
Suit: EARTH

COMPANION CARDS:
*The Well, The Point,
Causality*

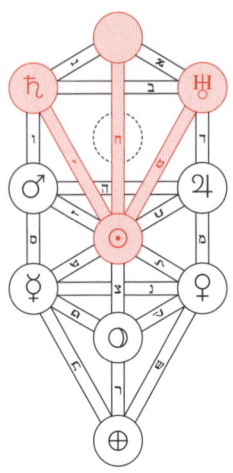

ORACLE

Does the minute grow into the huge? Does the acorn contain the microcosm of an oak? Or does the shell contain just the idea of a great oak tree? The male seed flows and penetrates the female egg, which then grows and uncovers a soul. What is that soul? A thing so vulnerable that it dare not whisper its own name. Tall and strong stands the grown man, and from his eyes blazes that which he does not know. For what is a man?

COMMENTARY

The everyday miracle of growth is a cause for wonder. At what point does the fertilized egg become a human being? Scientists, doctors, priests and astrologers all have their different viewpoints. Here physical development, faith, value and meaning are intertwined, and no one has the final word on what makes up a human being. Every time one view becomes prevalent, fresh discoveries open up the field again. Today's genetic research was yesterday's science fiction, but, however far we advance, the moral questions remain, as do the metaphysical ones. The Kabbalah is a tradition of analysis and argument, so it is well suited to taking on new challenges. Students of Kabbalah traditionally hammer away at texts, coaxing out secrets and revelations from them.

There is always an outer surface and an inner meaning, and this helps to keep our curiosity alive. In a living, growing creation nothing has a final explanation; it is an illusion to think we have reached the ultimate truth. In creation, the physical and the spiritual worlds are linked, and we have to wrestle to come even part of the way towards understanding how they interact. The Tree of Life is a tool for this: it provides a map of how these worlds connect and a ladder so that we can climb from the lower to the higher realms. But when we have reached the heights, where is the greater and where the lesser? What is small and what is large? What is inner and outer, higher and lower? All ladders and maps help us through secure steps and graded understanding. When ultimately the place of attainment is reached, it is no place at all, and the ladders and maps must be thrown away.

INTERPRETATIONS

Life tasks: *When you have set your course, you can allow growth to take place. If you have created the right conditions, it will flourish. Tend it with care and love: it will respond, because everything in our world has its own kind of life. You do not need to exert absolute control; trust works wonders.*

Possible meanings: *A new beginning. Conception. A seed begins to sprout. Something is alive and growing, but its future is as yet unknown. A complex situation. The need for trust and confidence. Higher teachings.*

THE CARDS

The Well גבא

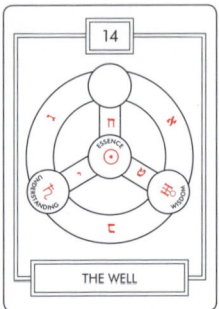

Wheel 14
Suit: WATER
COMPANION CARDS:
*The Covering, The Point,
Causality*

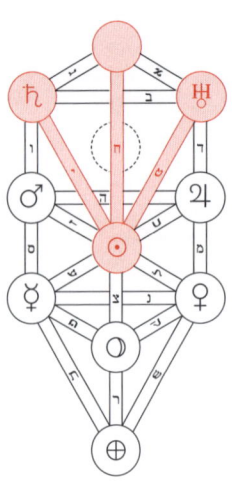

ORACLE

The depth of the well is unfathomable, and the rope upon which the bucket is suspended is infinitely long. And as the bucket is lowered into the well, it will knock the sides of the well, sending stones and moss tumbling into the deep, still water. There they will splash, soak up moisture and ooze with life. As each drop is tasted so is the well is refilled. For he who drinks of the well causes it to be replenished.

COMMENTARY

There is a gift of life which all of us possess. The waters of life flow and usually replenish our resources naturally. If we take physical rest and food and allow new impressions to feed our imagination, we soon regain vitality. Often, we simply need time for the waters to bubble up and fill the empty reservoir again. After a period when life has seemed meaningless, suddenly we hear the birds singing and enjoy the greenness of new leaves once more. The waters of life are irrigating the desert. But if this doesn't happen of its own accord, we need to seek those waters, and perhaps to clear the mud and debris that is obstructing them. The journey to the depths may be perilous – it is often described as travelling along a long rope or axis. Ancient societies knew how demanding this journey could be and often appointed a priestess or shaman to travel there on behalf of the whole community.

Through practices such as meditation and visualization, we can come to understand the process better and make the journey less difficult. These practices help us to know the source of the flow and when to let matters alone or when to take action. This means that in times of trouble we can reach the waters if we need to and slake our thirst. And the waters are inexhaustible. You can drink as much and as often as you like. An unused well is a stagnant well; regular use keeps the waters sweet and clean. No one is perfect – the clattering pebbles falling because of our clumsiness irritate and upset us, but they are a part of the life process too, and may start a whole new chain of events.

INTERPRETATIONS

Life tasks: *You have rich resources; don't be afraid to use them. But you may have to explore the hidden depths in order to release the energy that you need. And in those depths, you may find something surprising, something concealed which should be brought to the light of day. Are you ready for an inner journey – maybe to the very centre of your being?*

Possible meanings: *Helping others. The need for rest. Replenishment and renewal. Healing. New growth. A process which can be relied on, but not fully understood. Good investments.*

THE CARDS

The Point   חטי

Wheel 14
Suit: FIRE
COMPANION CARDS:
The Covering, The Well, Causality

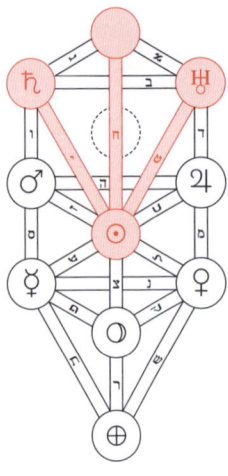

ORACLE
From the point, all conception extends as it grows. Its angles and surfaces, its dimensions and formations only become manifest as the point rests. From being the active initiator, it becomes the forgotten and hidden centre point of creation.

COMMENTARY
Creative energy is a great puzzle to us, especially, it seems, to the most creative artists and writers, who never know quite where their inspiration comes from. Although we can aid our own creativity, we can never ultimately command it. It lies embedded in the covenant between us and the creator; its presence can be known, but not fully revealed. In Kabbalah, the 'points' of creative growth are seen as the fiery sparks that fall like a shower of meteorites through creation. They kindle our vision and inspire us to new activity. Many spiritual teachings can also be found in everyday versions, so it is no surprise that we often talk about an idea being 'sparked off'.

Creativity is not only for the talented. It is not only about art, music and invention. It is to do with living imaginatively and richly, and finding new solutions to the challenges of everyday life. Creativity makes its way into every nook and cranny of life, it even produces new ways of working mechanically, resulting in cars, computers and all kinds of machinery. Creativity is impatient: it seeks quicker results and freedom from repetition. This in turn opens up new terrain to be explored and brings to light new problems requiring solutions. So creativity perpetuates itself.

But no one can live entirely at that point of creativity. Even trying to sustain the energy of creativity is against its very nature. We all have to be grounded in the physical, repetitive round of daily life, which brings other benefits – stability, love and solid achievement, for instance. But we also need to recognize the potential for creativity, and not dismiss an opportunity to use it. It is important to look beyond the pressures and demands of routine and have the confidence to take our own initiatives.

INTERPRETATIONS

Life tasks: *You are at the point of taking a creative initiative, whether you know it or not. Allow space for this to emerge; do not take on more routine tasks than you need to. Though you cannot tease a new idea out before its time, you can recognize and respect the hidden gestation that is taking place and be ready to give it form when it emerges. Such moments are precious; keep the memory of the creative spark in mind and it will help you when times are bleak.*

Possible meanings: *Creative activity. A discovery. The arts. A new impulse. A source of energy still in its early stages. A sexual attraction. The possibility of a new relationship.*

THE CARDS

Causality אגב

Wheel 14
Suit: AIR

COMPANION CARDS:
The Covering, The Well, The Point

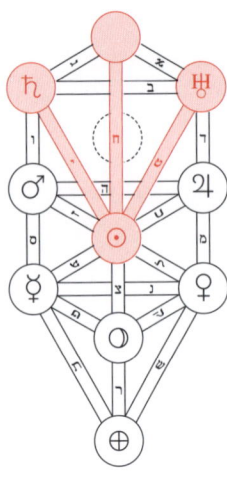

ORACLE
What is causality? The philosophers may argue over its absolute nature, but we know something at least of its capabilities. It multiplies, and disseminates, as it manifests within time and space. It can only be known by its products, which are reflected in the myriad hues of existence. And these change like the shapes of clouds blown by the wind through the sky.

COMMENTARY
The forms that we know change over time, sometimes abruptly, sometimes slowly. Everything is ultimately in a state of change and flux: countries and continents merge and drift apart; mountains are thrown up and slowly crumble away. Floods and earthquakes produce sudden and dramatic changes, while in the human world, wars shape the fate of a nation and revolutions of thought and belief create an equally profound change in the mind of humanity. It can be agony to recognize and acknowledge change. Even our own beings are changing and ageing, and will one day cease to exist.

When we can accept change, then we are ready for higher knowledge. Ignorance of change means that we erect a barrier, saying that everything depends on this one form, this present body, this current idea, and that if this should be lost, then all is lost – there is nothing more. Recognition of change means that we can move beyond these limited views and ask: What is the nature of spirit? What are the real qualities of mind? What principles is the universe created on? For although the forms themselves change, the principles remain. This is not idle debate if we really engage in it. It takes courage to make that leap of understanding, because we fear leaving behind all that we know and love. But love is also present in the realm of causality. The unknown is potent, but need not be feared.

Eventually, through knowledge, comes a new humbleness. We cannot know it all. But what does that matter? The path that is no path is open before us; there is always more to discover. The footprints of those who have been there act as guidance, and the great glyphs such as the Tree of Life teach us how and where to look.

INTERPRETATIONS

Life tasks: *It is not enough just to keep going; you need to examine why and how the situation has arisen. This gives you a chance to master it, rather than being driven by it. Take time to reflect; create the space to consider, even when you are in the middle of activity. Perhaps it is time to shake off your old ideas.*

Possible meanings: *An explanation which reveals the truth of a situation. The root cause. A way forward. Study of philosophy or spiritual matters. Abstract design or calculation; forward planning. The reasons behind a decision.*

READING THE CARDS

This oracle pack is a divination system. You can ask it a specific question or opt for a general reading, which usually focuses on an individual and their current circumstances. If it is a particular question, the questioner must be able to frame it in words. It can be about a practical everyday issue or about something with a more emotional or spiritual content. But remember, it can be a lot easier to deal with mundane questions – the spiritual elements often reveal themselves within the practical issues anyway.

It is usually best to do the reading with the other person physically present, especially when the oracle is still new to you. It helps to create the conditions in which the oracle is likely to work at its best. It is debatable whether it is ever advisable to do a reading for yourself, because the more involved you are with the question, the harder it is to let the cards speak to you. Even when you are giving a reading for someone else, try to distance yourself from your feelings about them. To give a clear reading, you have to go beyond your normal judgements. Then you will have the chance to reach a place of knowledge.

In a reading, the meaning of each card arises out of its general significance, combined with its context and the house it *falls in (determined by the space where it lands on the reading sheet). You will see this in the sample reading which follows. But each card is also a part of the whole reading. It is very important to survey the layout as a whole, to ponder its overall character and to allow your intuition to guide you in interpretation. Oracles are inspirational, as well as functional.*

Divination is primarily about the present, not the future. The future arises out of the present, and often the insight we gain into the current situation helps us to see what direction the future is likely to take. The cards may certainly suggest events which are still to come, but be careful and gentle in the way you communicate these. Like any method of divination, your readings will always be an interpretation, not absolute truth. Insight into the present may give the person concerned a chance to change the future.

You are now entering a very old tradition, connecting with the lineage of those who have sought knowledge through the Kabbalah. The leaves on the Tree of Life are the cards of this oracle. Use them truthfully and compassionately and you, in turn, may receive wisdom from them.

The Tree of Life and the Reading Sheet

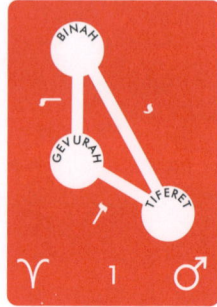

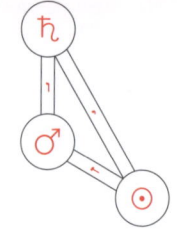

The sheet layout is a version of the Tree of Life. Each card space corresponds to a triad on the Tree, with a sefira at each corner. You can relate these and the Hebrew letters to the Tree of Life as shown here. In the Oracle, each of these twelve outer positions also corresponds to an astrological house, established by aligning the planetary rulerships of the sefirot and the astrological houses. With a few slight variations, it works as follows: for example, the first house in astrology corresponds to Aries, the first sign of the zodiac. Aries is ruled by Mars; Mars is placed at Gevurah. So the triad assigned to the first house is one of those which includes Gevurah.

The houses in astrology are often called the 'mundane' houses. They are a kind of practical, everyday version of the twelve zodiac signs. For example, Taurus, the second sign of the zodiac, is a lover of material things, so the second house rules money and possessions. If you want to find out more about the houses, any good book on astrology will tell you. It is helpful to have a basic grasp of them to use this oracle pack, because they will give you the context in which each card will reveal its meaning. The twelve houses make up the complete sphere of human life; any activity or issue that arises can be ascribed to a house, and with practice you will see how to do this. There are keywords included on the sheet to help you, and more detailed descriptions opposite.

The two central positions on the sheet, the Significator cards S1 and S2, relate to the core of the situation. The First Significator (S1) represents its essence, and often shows why the question was asked and what state the questioner is in. The Second Significator (S2) gives guidance as to the best way to act and how the situation is likely to change.

TIME FRAME

You will find attributes of time beside each house on the reading sheet. These give a time frame which you can use as necessary. For example, you may be asked a question which is very dependent upon a sequence of events, and this can help to clarify what has already happened and what is likely to happen next. Or you may like to do a time scan of the reading after you have done a house-by-house interpretation. Sometimes you will not want to use the time frame at all, but it is there if you do.

HOUSE	MEANINGS
First house	*Initiative, beginnings, impulses, appearance, energy level*
Second house	*Possessions, money, comfort, desires and pleasures*
Third house	*Communication, study, skills, brothers and sisters, short journeys*
Fourth house	*The home, childhood, the mother, roots, security*
Fifth house	*Lovers, creativity, gambling, speculation, art*
Sixth house	*Health, work, administration, detail, ritual*
Seventh house	*Partners and one-to-one relationships, enemies, legal matters*
Eighth house	*Sex, death, mystery, deep feelings, savings and storage*
Ninth house	*Long journeys, philosophy, religion, higher education, aims and ideals*
Tenth house	*Profession, the father, ambition, status, long-term plans*
Eleventh house	*Friends, society, networks, social activities, discoveries*
Twelfth house	*Enclosed places, hospitals, secrecy, deception, dreams*

READING THE CARDS

How to Lay Out a Reading

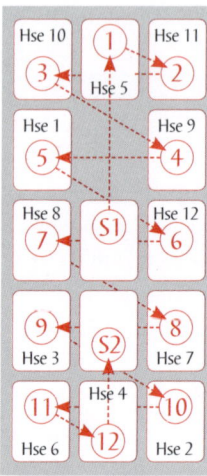

This shows the order in which to lay out the cards, as shown by the circled numbers above and on the sheet. Begin with the First Significator S1, then follow through 1–12, ending with Second Significator S2 as your last card. Also shown here is the order of the houses, as indicated on the sheet.

The Questioner is the one who is consulting the Oracle and the Reader is the person who is interpreting it.

STEP ONE To begin, the Reader asks whether the Questioner has a specific question or would like a general reading. A specific question can be revealed now or later in the reading. The Oracle is not designed to be a test of psychic ability though, and it is usually helpful to know the question at the start.

STEP TWO The Questioner then shuffles the pack thoroughly. While this is going on, both Reader and Questioner should remain calm and relaxed. The question can be floated gently in the mind, but without any intense emotional engagement.

STEP THREE When the Questioner feels that the cards are shuffled enough, the Reader takes the pack and cuts it once with their left hand (or with the right hand if he or she is left-handed), replacing the cards so that those that were at the top are now at the bottom. Then he or she fans out the cards face down and the Questioner picks one out. The Reader places this face up on the central position of the First Significator S1.

HOW TO LAY OUT A READING

STEP FOUR The Questioner then cuts the pack with the left hand (or vice versa as Step Three) and replaces the two halves in reverse order. This process is repeated twice more, so that the pack is cut and reassembled three times altogether.

STEP FIVE The Reader lays out the twelve cards of the houses face up, taking them in order from the top of the pack. But they are not laid out in the order of the houses. They are laid in the order of the Lightning Flash on the Tree of Life, as shown opposite and in the circled numbers on the sheet. The other numbers indicate the house each card space represents.

STEP SIX The Reader fans out the remaining cards and the Questioner picks another single card to be the Second Significator S2. This is placed on the sheet. The reading is now ready for interpretation.

The Blank Card

This is shuffled along with all the other cards. If it turns up as the First Significator or in any of the twelve houses, the reading is invalid. (As the Second Significator, it is fine, and means that possibilities for action are wide open.) If this happens, ask the Questioner if they really want this reading and are ready to listen to what it says. As the Reader, ask yourself if you have any desires or prejudices that might distort your interpretation. When you both feel that you have cleared the obstruction, you can start again from the beginning. If the blank card comes up three times in a row, do not proceed with the reading – try again another day.

Other Ways of Using the Cards

You can draw just one card, to give an immediate reading. Use the 'Life tasks' section as a key to interpretation. You can also do a three-card reading, which will give you the dynamics of any situation, or a four-card layout, which gives you the essence of the matter and its dynamics.

139

READING THE CARDS

Sample Reading

Tamara is a woman in her thirties who runs her own company. Lately, financial problems have held up her business plans and she has put her personal life on hold while she is dealing with these.

We agreed to do a general reading, as I felt it would be more helpful to look at the situation as a whole rather than focus exclusively on work.

As with every reading, you must sometimes follow your intuition, especially when you cannot immediately see which of several topics the card might be referring to. For instance, the twelfth house can be about secrecy, but in this case I decided that the card probably related to the immediate future, one of the 'time-frame' meanings that each card has. I also look at a card in the context of the whole reading, which sometimes colours an individual card.

When you give a reading, look also at its overall contours and features. Which of the four elements is most strongly represented out of earth, water, fire and air? These will tell you whether you are dealing with mainly a practical, emotional, creative or mental issue respectively. What stresses, harmonies and breakaway factors can you see in the layout? These indicate the unique characteristics of a reading.

I usually approach a reading by quietly contemplating the layout for a few minutes, and then I interpret the First Significator before I go through each house in turn. That is followed by the Second Significator, and afterwards I return to the reading as a whole to see if it now gels in a particular way. I also ask the person if there are any more questions arising out of what I have already said. But it is important to know when to stop, so that the energy of the reading doesn't dissipate. Make it a definite statement: return the cards to the pack and put away the sheet. Don't answer any further questions or speak your belated thoughts; they may distort the truth once the space for the reading is closed.

Here are the main interpretations I came up with for Tamara.

SAMPLE READING

SIGNIFICATOR – THE HEAD
You need to keep everything in a compact and tight framework at the moment. This will make it easier to keep control of your options in a difficult situation.

1ST HOUSE – THE MARTYR
On a day-to-day level, your resources are being wasted in a number of different ways. You need to pay attention to detail as well as to the big picture. Check your procedures and tighten them up if necessary.

2ND HOUSE – THE SLUGGARD
It doesn't look as though there is going to be any immediate improvement in your finances. The situation is slow to resolve. All you can do is to protect what you have and wait for a change in circumstances.

3RD HOUSE – THE EATER
You are hungry for developing new ways of communicating and selling your products. At the moment, your approach may be costing you plenty without providing much return, but you could turn that around. Why not look into different forms of advertising, for instance?

4TH HOUSE – THE WELL
The first cards were not promising, but here the picture changes. You have a connection back to your childhood and your roots which really sustains you. The waters from it run clean and clear. It gives you an enviable inner security.

5TH HOUSE – THE OBSERVER
Because you haven't been able to follow your plans through, you have developed the art of watching and waiting. You are waiting until the moment is right to take a gamble. This has made you very observant

and shrewd. However, it is also blocking off your creativity, and you should consider launching yourself into some really stimulating activity.

6TH HOUSE – THE RETURN
This is a very rich card and draws from many resources. It suggests that you should rally all your skills, especially those you've developed in the past. You can start working in ways you've almost forgotten about; you haven't lost those skills and you need to re-assess them now.

7TH HOUSE – CONCERN
This house was a bit of a puzzle to us both, as Tamara doesn't currently have a partner. However, it could mean that there soon will be strong concern over a close friend, who will require her help and attention. It could also mean that a minor current legal dispute could take on far greater significance than it has at present.

8TH HOUSE – THE MYTH
Rather than waiting for the right sexual relationship to come along, you should throw out some of your old dreams and fantasies and be awake to the possibilities here and now. You may be in thrall to an archetype of sexuality which is no longer appropriate for you.

9TH HOUSE – THE ACTOR
However you portray your feelings about spiritual matters to others, be sure you are sincere with yourself. There is a danger of the play-acting taking over the actor, and of forgetting to honour that sacred connection.

10TH HOUSE – THE VICTOR
This card gives real cause for optimism, suggesting that you will eventually triumph over all your current difficulties. You are in charge of the game plan and have a great deal of strength.

11TH HOUSE – PRIDE
Your friends are a source of pride to you. You say that you have only a few close friends – perhaps they are like a 'pride' of lions! You may not be overtly sociable, but your connection in to a network is strong.

12TH HOUSE – THE UPROOTED
Change will come soon and suddenly. It may throw you off balance, but if you keep control of your existing enterprises, you can steer your way successfully through it. But the change that you experience won't necessarily be on your own terms.

SECOND SIGNIFICATOR – THE AUDIENCE
Whatever you decide to do, tell other people about it. Get opinions and advice. Communication is an important factor right now for making progress. Tell your staff too, and make sure that they listen. Get the channels of communication really working well.

Overall Impressions

Tamara would like a major external change which will set her fortunes to rights and bring all her hard work to fruition. The reading suggests that change is coming, but probably in a rather disruptive way and she will actually have to control its impact carefully so that it does not fragment the structure of her work and life.

Rather than holding fire on the creative and relationship front, Tamara should activate those areas now. If she releases some of her sexual and creative energy, this may help her situation in general. She has a strong sense of direction, but needs to realize that neither her own careful planning, nor an unknown external change can completely implement it. Liberating her own energies may be what is needed, even though they are unpredictable, and doing this involves a certain amount of risk.

Acknowledgements

Author's Acknowledgements
The original Oracle sections of the texts for each card have been included and adapted with the kind permission of Eddie Prevost, who contributed these to *Galgal – The Master Game*, published by Scot o' the Covert in 1972. Thanks go to Gila Zur, who generously allowed me to take the original design of the Oracle forward into its current form and who has participated in its rebirth with enthusiasm. Her checking of all Hebrew letters and words has been invaluable in this edition.

I would like to pay tribute to the tradition of Kabbalah, which gave birth to this Oracle, and which provided my own much-valued training ground. I would also like to acknowledge the Saros tradition of knowledge, which encourages us to question and to open up new channels for creative wisdom to flow through. Without the old tradition, there is no substance; without new exploration, there is no fresh discovery.

Eddison Books Limited would like to thank Helen Jones for her valuable contribution in recreating the card illustrations for this new edition.

Commissioning Editor: *Liz Wheeler*
Editors: *Nicola Hodgson, Jo Weeks*
Proofreader: *Jo Weeks*
Creative Director: *Nick Eddison*
Art Director: *Elaine Partington*
Design: *Braz Atkins*
Book Illustrations: *Braz Atkins*
Production: *Gary Hayes*